THE COURAGE TO BE YOURSELF

*A Woman's Guide
To Growing Beyond
Emotional Dependence*

by

SUE PATTON THOELE

PYRAMID PRESS
P.O. BOX 1480
NEVADA CITY, CA 95959

First Edition

Cover design: Robert Steven Pawlak

Library of Congress Cataloging in Publication Data
    Library of Congress Number 87-63397
    Thoele, Sue Patton
    The courage to be yourself.
    1. Woman — Psychology
    2. Self-Help
    ISBN 0 - 961 9845 - 0 - 3 Soft Cover

Published May, 1988
Second Printing, January 1989
Third Printing, September 1989
Fourth Printing, March 1990

Dedication

**In loving memory of
my courageous mother,
Virginia Faris Patton,
who had a special talent
for listening.**

Acknowledgements

Thank you to Bonnie Hampton for walking the first miles of this book with me and steadfastly believing I could "go it alone". Thank you to Joyce McKay, Polly Ostrofe, and Irene Frazier for their insightful expertise, gentle suggestions, and valuable time. Thanks to Paul Kelly, Helen Strang, Bella Potapovskaya, and the late Catherine Kielhorn who patiently "put it all together". Extra special thanks to Gene Thoele for all his love, support, and enthusiasm . . . and because he is fun to live with!

Introductory Note

For the inspiration they have given me, I wish to thank each of the writers whose words I have quoted here.

In the notes at the end of the book I have supplied as much bibliographic information as I could obtain. Full information is missing from some citations: quotations treasured over the years but long since separated from their source.

TABLE *of* CONTENTS

PART ONE
The Courage To Be Yourself

PART TWO
Facing The Dragons In The Dungeon

PART THREE
Unresolved Grief:
Drowning In Life's Debris

PART FOUR
Limits And Boundaries:
"I Have Rights!! Okay?"

PART FIVE
Healing: Owning Your Own Excellence

Part One

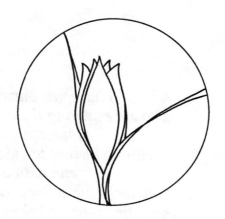

The Courage To Be Yourself

*I have met brave women
who are exploring the outer edge
of human possibility,
with no history to guide them,
and with a courage
to make themselves vulnerable
that I find moving beyond words.*

—GLORIA STEINEM

Introduction

THIS BOOK IS ABOUT courage, and it was born out of my struggle to become an independent woman, to create my *own* feelings of emotional well-being instead of relying on other people or circumstances to give me my peace of mind. At the time when I began my journey, I was feeling that life had given me much less than I had dreamed I'd get. I felt ripped-off, cheated, and used. Knowing that I often felt insecure, dependent, and inadequate even though I appeared independent and successful, I began a quest to have my inner feelings match my outer appearance.

My search began when, at age thirty-one, I became a single parent with no means of support. Life had, effectively, given me a good hard shove toward independence. I returned to graduate school to study counseling psychology, which proved to be a life-changing path for me.

I began to learn who I was in my own right, rather than as a reflection of circumstances and other people. I gradually moved beyond self-definitions such as daughter, mother, or one half of a couple—and discovered what I, uniquely, feel and am capable of doing.

Even after becoming a professional therapist and remarrying, I continued to be plagued by feelings of dependence. It became increasingly obvious to me that, in fact, my emotional dependence was being created and continually regenerated by my fears. When I read Colette Dowling's book, *The Cinderella Complex: Women's Hidden Fear of Independence*, many of those fears boiled to the surface. Over the months and years that followed, I struggled to free myself from the tyranny of fear.

The turmoil and triumph of my battles with fear have given birth to small growth groups for women, which I've led together with my partner and friend, Bonnie Hampton. Our work has centered on the common fears and emotional dependencies of women, and these groups in turn evolved into a seminar titled: *Beyond Cinderella: the Courage to Be.*

From our struggles and those of the courageous and inspiring women in our groups, seminars, and private practices, came this book. In it, I will share with you what we have found to be healing, creative, and freeing.

Every one of the true stories and case examples related in the book describes an important stage in one woman's experience of learning to be herself. In the stories you will find proof that we women *can* have the courage to be uniquely ourselves—that emotional independence is, in fact, our birthright, our privilege, and our responsibility. As we find the freedom to express who we really, uniquely are, we create a climate around ourselves in which others can also grow and be healed.

My hope in writing this book is that, in the pages that follow, you'll find many ideas and exercises that will help you find the Courage To Be Yourself and to discover the joy of expressing who you really are.

This book contains no pat answers because your path to inner freedom must unfold uniquely from within *you*. But each of the exercises is designed to help you find *your own* way toward increased independence. If writing helps you clarify your thoughts and feelings, I would love to hear from you. You can write to me in care of Pyramid Press, P.O. Box 1480, Nevada City, CA 95959.

We women are wonderfully courageous: we have what it takes to tame our fear-full inner dragons. I have slain many of my own and have watched in awe as many other women courageously overcame obstacles and traumas that had once nearly destroyed their faith in themselves.

You have just as much courage as these women have! Take heart. Be patient. Don't try to go it alone. Live gently with yourself and others as you start on, or continue, your inner journey.

But the whole point of liberation
is that you get out.
Restructure your life.
Act by yourself.

—JANE FONDA

CHAPTER 1

Courage:
You Can Have It!

YOU ARE ALREADY courageous! The very act of reading a book such as this, which is full of challenges to growth and change, is courageous.

Many of us are caught in the tangled web of emotional dependence. We look to others for our happiness, our "self"-concept, and our emotional well-being. We give up what we want and need out of fear of rejection, abandonment, or confrontation. Being emotionally dependent puts us at the mercy of our fears and other people's whims. We are not free to be ourselves. It takes an enormous amount of courage to be emotionally independent.

Having the courage to be who you really are is your natural birthright. What is courage? It's the willingness to risk or act even when you are frightened or in pain. Courage is the ability to do what needs to be done, or feel what needs to be felt, in spite of fear. Perhaps you want to be emotionally independent and have more courage. You can!

Unfortunately, many of us have allowed fear to block our awareness of our inborn strengths. I myself used to be a master at doing that. Although other people perceived me as an independent person, I frequently felt I was only playing at being grown up. Others saw me as successful and mature, but I wasn't fooling myself; inside, I felt buffeted by other people's moods, a helpless leaf in any storm. I knew that I hadn't taken responsibility for my own life, and I was afraid to do so.

Even though I had a master's degree in counseling and had been in private practice for several years, inwardly I felt I was "just a wife and mother." Sure, I had performed the work of an adult person, leading groups and seeing clients, but inside, I felt like a little girl dressing up like a grown-up and playing at these roles, hoping to gain the approval of others.

What changed? A great deal! I turned 40, met a wonderful woman friend who wouldn't let me lie to myself, and, most importantly, I began to *really* listen to myself. Each of us has a "still, small voice" inside that speaks to us continuously. The trouble is, we seldom listen. Yet, if we let it, our inner authentic self can guide us unerringly. You, too, can hear that voice, which will help you to have the Courage To Be who you really are.

We seldom think much about the courage we exert in simple, "normal" situations: having a baby, going to work day after day, having relationships. It takes courage to fall in love, to be honest with yourself, to survive a loss, to move away from home, to share a fear with a friend, to ask for a raise, to get a divorce, to take on a job that challenges you, to tell someone when you're angry or hurt. Try writing down a list of things you've done even though you felt afraid. Those were acts of courage. Sometimes just getting up in the morning and proceeding with your life takes tremendous courage!

So, as I hope you can see now, you *have* courage. Being courageous, and moving toward a fuller realization of our own authentic self, is a natural process. What is it that keeps us from realizing our full potential? *FEAR!* What do we fear? We fear the unknown. We fear anything that has been painful for us in the past. Anything that feels different, or risky.

But risk has an entirely different side, too. With the right attitude, you can experience risk as exhilarating and creative. Risk is necessary for change, and change is necessary for growth. Growth is inevitable! We *will* grow, but will it be toward freedom or fearfulness? In order to be free we need to learn to honor our fears but not allow them to control our lives.

Bringing our fears out into the open and talking honestly about them helps us work through them. An unspoken fear is much more powerful than one which is shared.

The trouble is, we're afraid to talk about our fears because we think others will see us as cowardly, immature, or foolish. So we keep quiet, thus creating a self-enclosed inner world in which we condemn ourselves for feeling as we do and believe we're the only fearful people we know. Our fear creates crippling isolation. But as we speak our fear and find it accepted gently by others, it loses its power. The most important thing the women in our seminars do is learn to talk openly about how they feel. As they share their shortcomings, secrets, fears, hostilities, joys, and disappointments with other women, they realize they are not alone. Breaking our isolation gives us permission to fully experience our feelings and then work through them.

Katy, a sweet, soft-spoken woman, sheepishly told me I couldn't possibly guess what she had discovered in one of our seminars. She was certain I'd be shocked and horrified to know that the main stress in her life related to her husband. Of course, I was neither shocked nor surprised, and *that* surprised her. I know her husband, and he's a good man; but I also know that many women who are in relationships with good men feel stressed in those relationships. In Katy's case, the mere reassurance from another woman that she wasn't alone in her unrevealed feelings, and that she wasn't a terrible person for feeling them, gave her the freedom to accept what she was *really* feeling.

Katy found acceptance of her feelings through a three-step process that I call a "Road Map Toward Being." First she became AWARE of her feeling, then with the help of another person she was able to ACKNOWLEDGE the feeling in its full dimensions, and finally, she was able to ACCEPT her feeling. Katy experienced a gentle and loving way to deal with her fear.

The rest of this book will guide you through steps by which you, too, can free yourself from fear and loneliness.

Women's Liberation

*We're not yet
where we're going
but we're not still
where we were.*

—NATASHA JASEFOWITZ

CHAPTER 2

Getting There: A Road Map Toward Being

ARE YOU SITTING beside your life's road waiting for someone to come along and give you a ride? People to take you on *their* trip? We women were taught to wait patiently for life. Some of our best tour guides were Doris Day and Rock Hudson, Ozzy and Harriet Nelson, TV programs such as "Father Knows Best"—and our own mothers.

Who ever heard of a damsel rescuing a knight in distress? We may *do* it all the time, but we were taught to *act* as if someone else were in the driver's seat of our lives. It doesn't work! The journey is our own.

No matter where we're going—to the supermarket, to work, to Europe, to a career, to marriage—we need maps to show us how to get to our

destinations. As women who seek to be free of emotional dependence, we, too, need road maps. In the
chapters that follow, I'll show you many maps that
have helped me find my way to greater inner freedom. I encourage you to use these maps gently and
tolerantly.

Road maps generally contain a large, overall map,
plus smaller maps of the cities in the area. I'll now
show you the "big map" for this book, which I call:

The Three A's Map

AWARE:	Become *aware* of your feel-ings. Inner awareness is the beginning of outer change.
ACKNOWLEDGE:	*Tell* a trusted friend or coun-selor about your awareness.
ACCEPT:	*Honor* where you are and what you are feeling. Give yourself a break! You're OK!

Now, let's look at the smaller, detailed maps for
the main principles we'll discuss in the book:

Become Aware

All change begins with awareness. Become
AWARE of what you're thinking and, even more important, what you are feeling; then you'll be able to
work with and *change* your feelings and actions. If

you're not aware of what you're feeling, the feeling will become your master. When you suppress or repress a feeling, you lose control over how you *express* it. And you *will* express it. It'll build up power until it can't be held in anymore, and most likely you'll express it in destructive ways. But if you become aware of your feelings early in the process, you can *choose* how to express them constructively.

It isn't always easy to become aware of your feelings. Many of us spend our whole lives trying to please others, without even thinking about it. Consider this poem by Roseanne, a career person with two children, a husband, and a difficult live-in father-in-law:

SATURDAY

The family has gone on an outing,
Responsibilities I've put on the shelf.
This Saturday I have been counting
On spending some time on myself.

But life is full of vexation.
That fact should have given me a
  clue
To expect unexpected complications
. . . I've forgotten what I like to do!

Roseanne had lost herself in constantly pleasing others. She felt depressed because she had repressed her own, unfilled needs. When she began to see that she, too, had rights, that she did not have to sacrifice herself on the altar of her family and her job, she also became aware of what she wanted and needed. In therapy she began to detach

herself from the old, burdening sense of responsibility for the lives of all the people around her. Now,
she feels free to make a life for herself and, consequently, feels *more* loving toward her family.

Warning! As you begin to honor your feelings
and needs, you may find others labeling you as selfish, or you may find yourself *feeling* selfish. Most of
us were taught *not* to be selfish . . . to think of others
first. Chapter 13 will help you see how you can be
less selfish if you do not deny your own feelings,
wants, and needs.

Another obstacle to greater awareness is the fact
that unawareness pays off in short-term, self-
defeating ways, by letting us ignore pain and anger.

Ruth's mother beat her when she "misbehaved"
or "spoke out of turn." Ruth learned to turn off emotionally, to become as invisible as possible, to detach
herself from people, and to avoid intimate relationships. As a child, those were survival skills; as an
adult, they give her great pain.

Ruth became so good at detaching herself from
her feelings that she actually did not feel the pain of
her mother's beatings. Today, the little girl inside
her, whom she still tries desperately to protect, is
afraid to get too close to people. As a result, Ruth
feels terribly isolated and lonely. What helped her
survive in the past keeps her separate in the
present.

Many of the choices we made when we were
young were wise at the time. In learning to deal
with our fears in new and more creative ways, we
should be very patient and gentle with ourselves.
It's not at all appropriate to feel guilty for childhood
patterns that may have helped us survive. After all,
when we made those early decisions, we were do-

ing the very best we could. And, in many cases, that was truly heroic!

Turn your attention to helping yourself choose new and lovingly positive ways of dealing with your fears and anger. The process of change takes time, so be gentle with yourself, and don't blame yourself for not changing overnight.

Awareness begins with an inner dialogue that goes something like this: "What am I feeling? When did it start? Where does my body hold it, in the form of tension? Is it a familiar feeling? How is this feeling limiting me? What is scaring me?"

Inner dialogue such as this helps you to stop blaming circumstances and other people for the hurts and disappointments in your life. It allows you to assume responsibility for your own reactions. More and more as you talk things over with yourself, you'll become able to sit in the driver's seat of your life.

The key is always to bring the responsibility back to yourself. You may not be able to change events, but you can change your reaction to them. "What am I doing? Why? Why am I saying this? How am I setting this situation up?"

The dialogue must be conducted gently. If you blame and verbally abuse yourself for problems and situations, you'll drown yourself in guilt, which will keep you from moving *through* uncomfortable feelings. Don't use "responsibility" as an excuse for beating yourself up emotionally. If you start to feel guilty, ask yourself, "Just *who* is demanding that I feel badly?" You'll probably run across an internalized critical-parent voice.

When we use dialogue, the person we're talking to is our inner, vulnerable child. If we're not careful to be very understanding and tolerant, our inner child will hide, and we won't be able to understand the choices she's making that are limiting her as an adult.

Becoming aware of feelings is like shining a light in the closet to make all the bogeymen and goblins run away. You may think, "Well, it's easy for you to talk about inner dialogue, but I've got so much junk buried away that if I open the door, it'll completely overwhelm me." But that's why you're reading this book: because it gives you practical tools for dealing with your fears in *manageable doses*.

In my work with women, I've discovered that we seem to have an inner control mechanism that doles out just about as many slimy toads and beasties as we can handle at a given time. The fear of being over-whelmed can hinder us by allowing us to *under*whelm ourselves and avoid facing our difficult feelings.

If you sense that you have hidden fears that threaten to erupt with volcanic force, by all means, see a therapist *immediately* before you begin to work on your own. Some people have repressed fears that can only be healed with patient professional help.

At times, you may need a strong, objective hand to hold. But most of us, most of the time, can parcel out our inner discoveries in manageable, "bite-size" pieces.

Acknowledge

The first step toward change is *awareness*; the next is acting on that awareness. ACKNOWLEDGE your new-found awareness fully. Fearful secrets separate us from others. They are like mushrooms . . . put them in a dark place, cover liberally with manure, and they will "mushroom!" Share your secrets with yourself first and then with someone who will listen nonjudgmentally. As we talk about our real and imagined shortcomings and our struggles to improve, we learn to forgive ourselves.

Too often, we create limiting feelings by speaking to ourselves in a judgmental, no-win voice: "You should." "You have to." "You shouldn't." Such words activate an internal response: "I won't!" "I can't!" To resolve this kind of internal "civil war," use words such as "could," "choose to," "want to," "can," "will," and "will not." This may seem like an overly simplistic technique, but it's not. Words such as "should" and "have to" imply that you have no power to choose in the matter. "Will" and "choose to" are words that free you to make conscious choices.

Have you ever said, "I feel sad," only to have someone retort sternly, "You shouldn't feel that way!" It stopped the conversation, didn't it? The connection with the other person was broken. Choose well the persons with whom you share your innermost feelings. You have a right to have your feelings, whatever they are. Painful feelings can only be transmuted and healed in a safe, accepting environment.

Learn to be a trustworthy friend yourself, and find friends and therapists whom you feel you can trust. Use your intuition in making these choices. You can only be honest in exploring your feelings if you don't fear the response of others.

Feelings are neither right nor wrong—they just are. When we're told we "shouldn't" feel sad or lonely or whatever, we will hesitate to open up again. This poem by Anais Nin expresses the importance of being gentle with ourselves and with our friends:

The value of the personal relationship
to all things is that it creates intimacy . . .
and intimacy creates understanding . . .
understanding creates love . . .
love conquers loneliness.
People only unmask themselves in the privacy
of love or friendship.
One has to treat them with care and tenderness.
Each is unique and we may never
see another like him.
We must protect him from injury
if we are to share his life.

Honestly and gently acknowledging our feelings and beliefs breaks the isolation and loneliness in which we live. We all need to feel understood and connected to others. In a climate of nonjudgmental love, we can truly become who we are meant to be.

There are many styles of acknowledging. My own style is to talk openly and honestly about my fears and the dark, nasty feelings I have inside of me. I process my feelings more quickly and efficiently when I speak them. If my feelings are out in the open, verbally hanging in the atmosphere, I can sort them out, understand them, and change them. Without the understanding of others, it takes me much longer to sort out my feelings. When understanding ears are scarce, I use my journal to talk to myself.

My internal process works best when it's externalized. Unexpressed, my feelings grab me by the neck and strangle me. It has been absolutely essential for me, in developing the Courage To Be Myself, that I find people who will hear me without judgment, and who will know with me that "this, too, shall pass." I sort as I talk, but other people have different styles.

Become aware of your most natural and comfortable way of acknowledging. What helps you to move toward being really you? Be flexible: experiment with what works and what doesn't. Develop a style that works for you.

At some point, it'll be important to acknowledge to someone other than yourself. It'll help reinforce your awareness, and feeling the acceptance of another human being will foster your own self-acceptance.

Accept

Do your best, even if you make apparent mistakes. How are you to judge if they are mistakes? You can only obey the higher urge which inclines you to contribute the best that you have to the service of the

community of men [women] and angels.
Thus, you shall be an ever-growing channel
for the light.

—The Quiet Mind

The third part of the road map is Acceptance. After you become AWARE of feelings and thoughts, and ACKNOWLEDGE them, you need to ACCEPT them.

Remember, feelings are neither right nor wrong; they just *are.* When you can accept your feelings just as they are, you'll be able to risk being honest outwardly. If you criticize and judge yourself for your feelings, you'll close down, hide, and relate less honestly to yourself and others.

Who likes to be browbeaten? How many times have you said, "I know it's so stupid, but I feel. . . ." or, "I know it's awful, but I feel like. . . ." Or (one of my old favorites), "Oh, you dummy! How stupid can you be?" If your feelings are always greeted by this kind of unloving, condemning dialogue, no wonder you don't want to express them!

Free yourself from old rules about right and wrong, and from judgmental self-talk. My own self-talk used to be excruciating. For instance, if I didn't like someone, I'd berate myself with such wonderful put-downs as: "Who are *you* not to like her? You're not so swift yourself!" or "You are only really a nice person if you love *everyone.*"

Now, when I have such feelings, I look at the feeling closely, check to see if there's a lesson I need to learn from it, confide in a friend if possible, and then tell myself something like: "It's okay, Toots. You don't have to like everybody."

Accept your feelings just as they are. In doing so,

you'll provide an inner climate that's conducive to growth and change. With acceptance, you no longer need to hide or pretend. You can speak out, bring the secrets out into the open to be transformed. Acceptance nurtures. Nurturing allows growth and flowering.

Honor where you are and what you are feeling. Then, if you choose, you can move on to something different. Give yourself a break! You're OK, and you're on the road to being "OKer."

Accepting yourself just as you are is an act of forgiveness: you forgiving you. Forgiving yourself also creates a mood in which you find it easier to forgive and accept others.

An excellent way to foster forgiveness and acceptance is visualization. Think about something that you dislike about yourself or something you wish you hadn't done. Say to yourself, "I did the best I knew how at the time. I am now willing to forgive myself." Visualize yourself putting whatever you regret into a basket attached to a beautiful helium balloon. Now take a deep breath and watch the balloon and basket float away. Let it go! Throughout your day, repeat the visualization. Tell yourself that you are now willing to release guilt and to forgive yourself. Don't expect to have instantaneous feelings of inner freedom and peace. Things held for a long time take time to be cleansed. Be gentle and patient with yourself.

Julie's story exemplifies the power of the "Three A's." Julie's mother was critical and abusive. In her therapy sessions with me, Julie *became aware* that she was trying to give me all the right answers, in order to avoid any possibility of my criticizing and judging her. She was trying too hard to please me (a mother figure) and be accepted by me. Later, she *acknowledged* this awareness to a personal friend, and they both *accepted* it without judgment.

In her next session with me, she spoke from such an honest place within herself, and it felt so completely natural, that she simply forgot to tell me about her new insight. At the end of our session, she realized that she hadn't been trying to please me or say all the right things. She then told me how using the Three A's had freed her from her initial fear of me.

Sometimes all it takes to change a behavior pattern is to *see* it and *say* it. Remember, *acceptance* of what you see and say is absolutely essential because only after you've accepted it can you move onward to *alter* whatever is limiting your freedom. Only then will you experience the inner feelings of authenticity that we all crave.

The Courage to Be Yourself is your birthright. You have all the tools within you that can enable you to express your*self* and your potential without being limited by fear.

Part Two

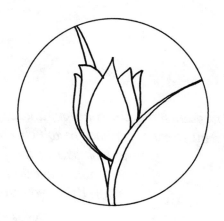

Facing
The Dragons
In The
Dungeon

You gain strength, courage, and confidence by every experience in which you really stop to look fear in the face. . . . You must do the thing you think you cannot do.

—ANNA ELEANOR ROOSEVELT

Fear

FEAR IS THE SINGLE MOST limiting factor in our lives. Fear binds us to hurts of the past and barricades our path to a fulfilled future. One of the main reasons fear has such power over us is that we try with all our might not to look at it.

Remember when you were a child and *knew* that a monster was leering out of the closet when you went to bed? But when your mom or dad (or you, if you were a brave soul) turned on the light, you found it was just a coat sleeve. What a relief!

The feeling of fear probably lingered, but you knew in your rational mind that the "monster" was a harmless coat. As adults, we sometimes try to hide our fears in inner closets, hoping that they, too, will disappear. "Out of sight, out of mind."

Unfortunately, out of sight and unattended to, our fears only grow larger. Fear feeds on darkness and secretiveness. When we refuse to look at our fears, they become very creative at getting our attention. In the next chapter, "Faces of Fear," I'll explore some of fear's creations.

If you open the closet door, turn on the light, and examine your fears, they stay manageable in size, and you *can* transform their energy for creative purposes. Many of us have learned to *beware* of fear instead of simply *being aware* of it. Awareness allows you to *choose* what to do with your fear. If you don't have the freedom to choose your actions, you're not in control of your life, and the boogie-persons in your closet are in the driver's seat. It's a rough ride, isn't it? Scary, too.

You *can* drive the vehicle of your life. Try it. Be AWARE of your fears. Boldly look in the closet and see what's there. Then, ACKNOWLEDGE those fears to yourself and to an understanding person. You'll be amazed when you discover how similar everyone's boogie-persons are. Finally, ACCEPT your fears. They may be uncomfortable, even terrifying, but once you can accept them and turn on the light in your inner closet, you'll gain the insight and ability to work with and transform them.

One of the reasons it's so difficult for us to look at our fears is that we were never encouraged to do so. We watched our parents deny their fears and then act them out in oblique ways. We learned to do that, too. We learned to project our fears outside ourselves. Instead of saying, "I get scared and feel abandoned when you raise your voice at me," we yell back in order to squelch the source of fear outside ourselves. Or we silently acquiesce, and then

feel angry and hurt inside. Either reaction only in-
tensifies our feelings of abandonment.

Fear isn't accepted in our culture. As children
we're allowed to be fearful up to a certain age, girls
somewhat longer than boys. But by the time we en-
ter school we're expected to have our fears under
control. Small wonder that when we feel afraid as
grown women, we hide our fear. The older we get,
the more clever we become at creating disguises for
our inner feelings.

We women are in a double bind: we fear failure,
but we also fear success. In relationships, we experience fear because of inner insecurity: we fear we're
not good enough, smart enough, slim enough, sexy
enough, caring enough. If we aren't earning
enough money, we fear that we're not doing our
part; if we make too much money, we're afraid that
we will threaten the men in our lives.

We fear we've done too much for our children,
thus spoiling them and making them dependent;
we fear we aren't doing enough for our kids and
that they feel neglected. When we're young we fear
that we haven't enough experience and credibility;
as we grow older, we fear the loss of our youthful
appeal.

Fear is generated as much by societal expectations, roles, and mores as by childhood experiences
and our reactions to them.

When we fail to look at our fears directly, they re-
semble dragons, hatching and gaining strength in
the dark cave of the subconscious. Growing quietly
away from the light, they eventually rise up over-
bearingly to demand our attention.

Freedom comes from knowing that fear can never
be avoided, but that it can be faced, lived through,

and learned from. Every time you face a fear, walk into the middle of it with support from others, a little bit of fear gets dissipated. Each time you challenge fear by doing what you fear, your fear diminishes.

Your unwillingness or inability to face the internal dragons of your fears doesn't prevent them from expressing themselves. They *will* express themselves, inevitably, but they'll wear disguises: the "Faces of Fear."

Fear is a question.
What are you afraid of, and why?
Our fears are a treasure house of self-
knowledge if we explore them.

—MARILYN FERGUSON

CHAPTER 3

Faces Of Fear

IF WE NEVER FACE our internal dragons of fear, they have the nasty habit of emerging from their caves in inappropriate and destructive forms. I call these unconscious and painful behavior patterns the "Faces of Fear."

Though fear wears many faces, I've chosen six for discussion here. I've experienced all of them, except overuse of alcohol and drugs. They're very common among the women with whom I work. Let's explore these fears and how we act as a result of them:

A ppeasing
F atigue
R esistance
A lcohol
I llness
D epression

Appeasing

Appeasing becomes, for many women, a familiar pattern. The dictionary defines "appease" as "to pacify; give in to the demand, either silent or spoken, of another." My own definition is "to try to make 'it' okay for the other guy, to take responsibility for his life, to placate at the expense of yourself and your feelings of self worth."

How often do you appease the man in your life by giving in to his moods and desires, even if it doesn't feel right for you? Or acquiesce to your children's demands when you really don't believe they're reasonable?

One of the reasons women are so prone to appease is that they need to feel connected to others. Carol Gilligan, the author of *In A Different Voice*, studied preschool children and found that even at that early age, girls were much more appeasing than boys. Girls wouldn't argue over the rules of a game but would try to make peace in order to preserve the relationships among their playmates. Boys needed to honor the rules of the game and would sacrifice closeness with their peers in order to maintain their stance. The author concluded that girls, more than boys, for whatever reasons, value emotional connectedness.

As adults, women seem to cultivate their need for emotional connectedness. We give ourselves away constantly, in order to feel connected to others; it's as if we feared *"Death by Disconnection."*

We try to appease people because we fear rejection, disapproval, and separation. Confrontation scares us: we feel uncomfortable when we disagree. Our stomachs churn and our throats get tight with fear. We fear that "they" may disagree with us, disapprove of us, dislike us, reject us, and even leave us. We dread feeling emotionally separated and abandoned.

Early in our lives, we learn to "make nice" in order to appease those with whom we want to stay connected. When we were children, our parents' disapproval felt life-threatening. As we grew older, we transferred our emotional, and sometimes economic, dependence from parents to peers, boy friends, mates, and government agencies.

Although women are making great strides toward economic independence, financial dependence remains a real need which often keeps us in unhappy and unhealthy situations. Even if we are independently wealthy, emotionally it often feels life-threatening to be out of favor with our mates, children, and friends. Through fear of emotional isolation, we too easily give up our independence.

Not only do women have a need for closeness, we've been trained by our society to be peacemakers. Many of us consider it our job to be emotional lighthouses for all those around us. Whenever someone seems to be in danger of going on the rocks emotionally, we feel it's our duty to jump in and rescue him/her. We appease in order to purchase "peace at any price."

Do you sacrifice your independence in order to keep the peace in your family or at work? If so, do you find yourself seething inwardly and feeling resentful and ripped-off? If you do, the price you are paying is lack of inner peace and low self-esteem. Quite a sacrifice!

Appeasing means giving ourselves away. Women often say in response to their own feelings, needs, and wants, or to a hurtful remark made carelessly, "Oh, well, I'll let that go. It's not worth the effort to deal with it." What you're really saying is, "*I'm* not worth the effort." We are the only caretakers of our feelings of worth. We teach people how to treat us! It's uncanny how, when we don't feel worthy, those around us see us as unworthy and begin to use us as emotional dishrags to clean up all messes. This kind of emotional dependence is excruciating. I know, because I used to be a chronic appeaser.

I was terrified of rejection. In my deep inner self, in the scared little girl I carried with me, I feared I would die if I were rejected. Through therapy, and through honest talks with myself and with friends, I learned to love and comfort my inner child whenever she felt rejected. Now I let her know she won't die, because she can always count on *me* to be there for her, emotionally.

I often see appeasing behavior in other women, especially in relation to their mates. I recently watched a friend try repeatedly to appease her husband. She had wanted to go to a concert, and they went together. During the performance, she kept checking with him to see if he was enjoying it. If she sensed that he was disgruntled, she would rub his back and talk cajolingly to him—as if to say, "Please, please enjoy yourself, so that I can enjoy myself." Later, she became AWARE of the fear that had prompted her behavior. Whenever her husband disapproves, he withdraws into icy moodiness. She felt that if he were bored, he would disapprove of her for having suggested that they go. Her life with him is a vicious circle: the fear of feeling rejected causes her to appease him, which in turn makes her mad at herself *and* at him.

Appeasing behavior is the negative face of a very powerful gift that women can offer to the world, which is to nurture people and make intimate connections with them. I've learned not to appease—but I *do* compromise. We need to compromise from a center of inner honesty and integrity . . . a place of strength and flexibility. That's a far cry from giving yourself away.

What to Do About Appeasing Behavior

The trick to changing appeasing behavior is to increase your tolerance for emotional separation. When you can learn to say, "Oh well, I see we'll be separate for a little while now. *How can I take care of myself in that time?*" then you'll have begun to break the chain that binds you to appeasing behavior.

What can you do when you feel rejected and need to strengthen your sense of self-worth? Call a friend. Go to a movie. Write in your journal. Talk to and take care of your inner child. Face your fears squarely, and then choose to stop the automatic, destructive behaviors they usually evoke. You will not die! You will survive!

Appeasing isn't an easy habit to break. The first step is to become AWARE of yourself when you are appeasing. When you think about appeasing, try to be very specific. Exactly how do you appease? And whom do you appease? Is it your husband, children, mother, or mother-in-law? When you become aware of appeasing behavior, stop and pay attention to how you feel. Like everyone else who appeases, you'll discover that you feel resentful, angry, and embarrassed.

Once you've become aware of your appeasing behavior, you can *choose* to act in different ways. The old yearning to appease will still be present, but as you continue to act in a respectful and authentic way toward yourself and others, the need to appease will gradually dissipate.

ACKNOWLEDGE your feelings to the person involved. If that isn't possible, or if it wouldn't be constructive, tell your feelings to a friend or to a therapist—even to your dog or cat, if necessary. Or, express them in a private journal.

ACCEPT the fact that you've been an appeaser and that you *can* choose to behave differently now.

Periods of change are full of paradoxes. They're difficult but exciting, frightening but freeing. Letting go of old patterns that no longer work for you is exhilarating. As you learn to replace appeasing behavior with assertive, self-valuing patterns, you'll begin to feel mature and equal in your relationships. Study the fears that keep you appeasing: look at them, examine them, bring them out into the open. As you learn about them, and consciously adopt positive counter-behaviors, your fears will dissipate, and you'll break out of the cycle of appeasement.

Fatigue

One of the quickest ways to feel tired is to suppress your feelings—to bury them in the dungeon of your subconscious. This process has been called "gunny sacking": anything you don't want to see or experience, you stuff into an emotional gunny sack, and as you hide more and more feelings, the sack gets bigger and heavier.

Small wonder that you feel fatigued—it's very tiring to carry around a big sack of fears, hurts, and disappointments, holding tight to the drawstring so they can't come out and overwhelm you. It's like sitting on a trap door through which many rebellious gremlins are trying to rise. If chronic fatigue is an issue in your life, it may be that some feelings need to be looked at and worked through. It's much harder work for your mind and body to avoid the feelings that need attention, stuff them down, ignore them, or put off dealing with them, than to face them. It takes an enormous amount of energy to hide from ourselves and others the dark feelings and thoughts we *all* have.

We say to ourselves, "Maybe if I ignore it, it'll go away." But of course it doesn't. Our unacknowledged feelings merely grow bigger, more ruthless and uncontrollable. In the long run, facing feelings is less work and infinitely more rewarding. Often, fatigue is a signal from our body and mind, telling us to be aware of hidden feelings.

Fatigue may indicate difficulty in one of four areas of our lives: physical, mental, emotional, or spiritual. In Chapter 13, in the section titled *"Nourishing from Overflow,"* I'll give a practical tool that will help you balance these four areas of your life. For now, let's look at the four areas themselves. I call them the four "quadrants."

PHYSICAL QUADRANT

My sons refer to their friends who lie around and watch TV as "Couch Potatoes." Have you become a Couch Potato? You'd be amazed at how much difference a fit body makes in how confident and capable you feel. Try to get at least 20 minutes of aerobic exercise four times a week. Give your body nutritious food. You cannot run (and most of us do, indeed, run) without effective fuel.

EMOTIONAL QUADRANT

What feeds you emotionally? Probably anything that increases your enthusiasm, your zest for life, your feelings of loving and being loved. Whether it's regular conversations with mates, friends, and children, a job well done, or heartfelt laughter—your emotions need nourishment. One of my own most effective emotional uppers is the ocean. I live 200 miles from the beach, but if I listen to my inner signals, I know when it is time to go and soak in the ocean's energy.

MENTAL QUADRANT

Just as the body and emotions need regular exercise and healthy "food," so does the mind crave the kind of nourishment it can get from inspiring, challenging ideas, books, and conversation. My admittedly biased theory is that too much TV destroys brain cells. Give up being drugged by T.V.! Shake the cobwebs out of your gray matter! Your brain can be a great ally in your battles with emotional dependence—and the brain thrives on exercise. Take a class, read a good book, work a crossword puzzle, or learn a sport.

SPIRITUAL QUADRANT

We are all spiritual beings. "Spiritual" in this context doesn't mean the same as "religious," although your religion can be very spiritual. Spirituality brings you peace of mind and a sense of being connected to a source higher than yourself. A walk in the woods, beautiful music, or sitting quietly may create a feeling of spiritual balance and harmony within you.

I find that in order to stay balanced, I must spend some quiet time every day with my special books and in prayer or meditation. Find out what feeds you spiritually, and make time in your schedule to practice it daily. Our spirituality is like water; we need it to survive.

Each of these four areas needs deliberate, conscious attention if we're to live as balanced, happy people. Be kind to yourself by honoring each of your four quadrants.

Begin also to become aware of the things you tend to stuff in your gunny sack. Pay especially close attention to the feelings that call themselves to your attention through fatigue. If you feel too threatened by your buried feelings to uncover them alone, seek professional guidance. Your fatigue is telling you it's time to lighten the inner load.

Resistance

It's human nature to resist what we fear. This face of fear, resistance, is quite clever: whenever we're challenged to change, it hides behind righteous indignation at how unfair and unfeeling people and circumstances are.

Some people resist *everything*—from the weather to ball scores to their spouses to politics. We think of such people as negative and grumpy; in reality, they're afraid. They fear everything that involves risk, change, or loss of control. Rather than look within themselves and change their own reactions, they blame the world outside.

The best way to overcome resistance is to be aware of it, acknowledge it, and then gently push on it. When you notice yourself becoming negative, laugh about it if you can. Magnify your gripes until they become ridiculous. The more lightly you deal with your resistance, the easier it'll be to move through it. Look at your resistance and, from the wiser, lighter part of your mind, choose to act anyway.

Resistance loves to put on disguises:

> *"I forgot . . ."*
> *"They didn't call me."*
> *"I overslept."*
> *"I'm too tired."*
> *"It doesn't matter anyway."*
> *"Why change? It's okay the way it is."*
> *"It's too hard."*
> *"I could never do that!"*
> *"You shouldn't feel that way."*
> *"That's dumb!"*
> *"Isn't it awful?"*
> *"I'm too fat (or too old) for that!"*
> *"I can't."*
> *"Why is it always me who has to change?"*

When I began to write this book, I came face to face with gigantic obstacles of resistance. After all, what did I have to say that would be worthwhile to anybody? Readers might laugh at my efforts. And just think of the sheer work involved!

My insecure inner self stepped forward sneeringly when I lost my tape recorder and the notes of my first meeting with my literary publicist. (I'd put them on top of the car, and they scattered all over the road.) I realized then that I was anxious about writing the book—terrified is a better word—and I spoke about it out loud. I honored the fear and didn't act on it. I stopped resisting the long process of writing the book, and promised myself I would take it one small step at a time. Working through my initial resistance was essential; if I hadn't dealt with it, I would never have completed the book.

Sharon, a client of mine, told me, "I've been really bothered by something you said last week." I had told her to gently look at any resistance she had toward therapy. She was convinced she wasn't resisting. She said she loved our time together; yet, she was 10 minutes late to her first session, and 20 minutes late to the second "because my husband wouldn't hurry." She missed the third session altogether, and was late again for the fourth.

As we talked about her behavior, she acknowledged that, yes, it was scary to come to therapy, and that she feared what she might find out about herself. Consciously, she was eager to learn and grow; subconsciously, she was frightened. As soon as she became *aware* of her resistance, she no longer needed to be late. She *acknowledged* her fears to herself and to me, and we both *accept* her resistance whenever it arises. She is learning to let fear go, piece by piece.

Resistance keeps us stuck in a narrow range of behaviors, thoughts, and feelings. Whenever we begin to push the boundaries of our "safe range," resistance plants itself firmly in our path. Going outside our "comfort zone" activates hidden fears of the unknown.

Resistance is a mistaken expression of a natural tendency. After all, there are many situations in which we really must protect ourselves. To strip away our healthy sense of caution suddenly and entirely would be like pulling off a protective scab. As you begin to work on your inner resistance, therefore, do so gently, patiently, and with love.

Alcohol

Women very often hide their fears in alcohol and drugs. If this is your problem, your first reaction will be, "Yes, I like (name your poison), but addiction isn't my problem." One of the major symptoms of chemical dependence is denial. Has this so-called non-existent problem evoked remarks from family and friends? Perhaps you should pay closer attention to what it is you're trying to deny.

I don't work with alcoholics or the drug-dependent, but I do work with the companion disease of alcoholism, called "co-dependency."

A co-dependent is someone who's in a relationship with a chemically dependent person. The "co" is addicted to the role of helper or caretaker. As we saw earlier, subservience to the needs of others is an effective way to mask your own fears.

One of the most self-destructive places to hide from fear and pain is in a bottle, a pill, or a line of white powder. What better way to mask your real inner feelings than to render yourself numb, unconscious, or artificially "high"? By wearing the mask of chemical dependence, you delude yourself into believing you're not responsible for working with your fears.

You aren't to blame for your fears, but you must make choices about how you'll handle them. You are responsible for making choices that are positive, healing, and constructive.

If you're hiding your fear behind a chemical mask, do yourself a life-saving favor: go to Alcoholics Anonymous. It's the most effective recovery program because it's a support system of people who've been where you are, who understand, and who *do* help.

Illness

Repressed feelings tend to lodge in the body, in the form of hidden tensions, unhealthy habits, and stress-induced chemical changes. Often, illness is an *ex*pression of feelings *re*pressed.

O. Carl Simonton and Stephanie Matthews-Simonton of the Simonton Cancer Center in Pacific Palisades, California found that when terminally ill patients expressed their gunny-sacked feelings of guilt, rage, fear, etc., their cancer frequently went into remission, or at least their symptoms became less acute. The Simontons' method of treatment includes techniques by which people become AWARE of what they're feeling, ACKNOWLEDGE it, and ACCEPT it.

We, too, seldom pay attention to the signals our intelligent physical body is sending us. When we ignore the signals, our body grabs our attention in creative ways. Chris's story is a perfect example. She was going through an extremely stressful divorce and felt depleted by the emotional strain. Her body was telling her to take time to rest and replenish her energies. She ignored its message and buried herself in work and other commitments, pushing herself to exhaustion.

A small cyst developed in her ear lobe; she ignored that, too. Her body had little choice but to send a more graphic message. The cyst enlarged until her ear was a painful and grotesque 2 to 3 times its normal size. With an ear *that* large, and being called "Dumbo" by her co-workers, how could she continue not to hear what her body was telling her? Her doctors said the cause of the cyst was stress. She got the message at last. As she began to *slow* down, her ear began to *go* down. Our bodies speak, sometimes even with subtle humor.

Illness can be a ploy that we use to get what we want or need without having to express it directly. If you're feeling unloved, under-appreciated, or scared, and you fall ill, your family must pay attention to you and cater to your needs. You can then feel nurtured and loved.

Illness is a fine way to resist. Who (including yourself) can expect anything of you when you're sick? Wayne is a good example. When he and his wife fight, he gets flu symptoms. He fears confrontation not only with her but also with his own feelings. By getting sick he avoids further confrontation. His unexplored feelings come out in the form of physical symptoms. Unfortunately, his inability to face his fears creates a lose-lose situation for himself and his wife. It spares him the discomfort of confrontation but leaves her frustrated, angry, and confused. He's left with physical symptoms, unresolved issues in his marriage, and he remains the uncomfortable target of her anger and frustration.

Our bodies talk to us, forewarn us, but we seldom listen. Several years ago, I was sick for 10 days straight—and I'm never sick. I ignored many clear warning signals, and finally my overworked body said, "Okay, Sue, you asked for it," and it just quit. I *couldn't* go on. For four or five days, all I could do was rest. Even reading was too strenuous. Later, I began to think, "Why did I need this illness?" It became obvious to me that I'd been feeling responsible for the lives of everyone around me. I'd convinced myself that my clients couldn't make it without me, and that my family needed my constant support, ever-wise counsel, and sense of humor.

Besides being an expression of a genuine desire to help my friends and family, my compulsion was an ego trip. I pushed and pushed—Wonder Woman flies again! But Wonder Woman finally fell into her bed and stayed there. Surprise! Everyone to whom I'd felt indispensable got along just fine. Clients survived, my professional life came back to normal very quickly, the family marched right along, friends took care of their own lives, organizations found other volunteers, and my body got its much-needed rest. Pattern broken!

An essential part of a happy, healthy life is being of service to others; but *indispensable is destructive*. Pace yourself in your work and commitments. *Nobody* is indispensable. Wonder Woman, hang up your magic bracelets! Use the techniques offered in Chapter 13 to help yourself stay on track.

The fear that led me to get sick was that if I didn't give my all, always, I wouldn't be good enough. Clients would leave, children would be neglected, husband would be disappointed—oh, horrors! I wouldn't be *perfect*! It took illness to show me that I'd reverted to two old patterns: (1) taking care of everyone else first; and (2) being perfect in order to be okay.

When you get sick, honor your body; give it the rest and medical attention that it's asking for.

Not all illness is emotionally induced. A therapist friend of mine who was used to self-evaluation developed a severe headache during her aerobics class. She asked herself all the usual questions: "Why do I need this? What am I not looking at? What do I need to learn from this headache?" No answers came. Was she hiding something from herself? Almost as an afterthought she loosened her headband. *That* worked!

Be gentle with yourself. If you discover that you're using illness as an escape, or pushing yourself until you get sick, learn to change that behavior. If your body gives out because it needs a rest, relax and enjoy it.

Depression

Depression is the classic disease of women. Why? Change two letters and instead of *de*pression you have *ex*pression. If we don't express what we're feeling—what's bugging us—*in a constructive, healing manner*, very often the result is depression: the way women weep without tears.

Depression is like a fog that settles over you, limiting your ability to see what you're really feeling. Often when we're depressed there's something we need to do about some situation, and we're afraid to do it.

Some kinds of depression are normal. When you experience a loss, a setback, a shattered dream, it would be unnatural not to feel a bit depressed. Depression is one of the five normal stages of grieving described by Dr. Elisabeth Kubler-Ross in her book, *On Death & Dying*. But most depression, and certainly chronic depression (unless due to some chemical imbalance), is a sign that you're hiding from something or avoiding action. And often, that "something" is anger.

In the psychology trade, there's an old cliche: "Depression is inverted anger." That's more or less true, but depression can also be inverted anything else. I don't know about you, but when I was growing up it was *not* okay for me to express anger. In our family, we denied that anger exists. I felt it, in myself and coming from my parents and sister, but we did not acknowledge it. We kept it locked in a closet, where it got bigger and bigger.

I remember giving in to anger once as a pre-teenager. Walking into my closet, I slipped in a little puddle that my sister had left on the floor. I swore. When I look back, I feel that it was reasonable anger and worthy of a good shout and a swear word or two. But my punishment for expressing my anger was being forbidden to attend a dance that I had looked forward to. Also, my mother wouldn't speak to me for the rest of the day. I learned to invert my anger to avoid rejection and punishment.

*Nice girls **don't** talk that way!*
*Nice girls **don't** act aggressive.*
*Nice girls **don't** rebel.*
*Nice girls **don't** get angry at people they love.*
*Nice girls **do** learn to play the victimized, poor-me*
role.
*Nice girls **do** learn to express their anger covertly,*
in manipulative ways.
*Nice girls **do** get depressed.*
*Nice girls **do** feel paralyzed by all their repressed*
feelings and their guilt about having such
feelings in the first place.

If you are depressed, check and see if, deeper, what you're really feeling is anger. Anger is natural—it's how you tell yourself, "Whoa, something isn't right here!" In our culture, anger and depression are labeled "bad." We believe a normal person must always be upbeat and happy.

We are only *really* depressed when we're not aware of our feelings. If we are aware of them and working them out, even if they are sad, we are in the very healthy process of healing.

Don't label yourself or allow others to label you as depressed if you are in fact experiencing your authentic feelings at the moment. I'm not talking about wallowing in self-pity—that's self-defeating. I am talking about taking out your fears and angers and looking at them. If you feel depressed, get specific: *What* are you feeling? Name it. Bring the dragon out into the light.

Marge was depressed and didn't know why. With gentle exploration, we uncovered her real feeling: sadness. She was sad over the realities of a marriage in which her husband wasn't able to understand many of her feelings and needs. She felt alone, frustrated, and unhealthy. She had covered her sadness and loneliness with vague depression because she feared that if she voiced her real feelings, she would leave him.

As a result of our working together in therapy, she discovered what she wasn't getting out of the marriage and set about finding ways to fill those needs for herself. She *chose* to stay in the marriage and concentrate on its many good aspects. She gave up her frustrated dependence on her husband, her expectation that he would fill all her needs; instead, she learned to work a computer, opened her own business, began to cultivate new relationships, and reconnected with friends she'd lost track of. Marge's depression was a valuable clue that she was covering up important feelings and limiting her life.

It's very hard for people to be on the receiving end of the full force of other people's anger. That's one reason why it's very important to learn to stop inverting your anger, holding it in until it comes out in self-destructive depression or in an uncontrolled volcanic explosion. Slugging your mate or kicking the dog is not constructive, but it is constructive to punch a punching bag, beat your bed, or play an aggressive game of racquetball.

If you don't allow yourself to become aware of your feelings, how can you express them? In Chapter 12 I'll talk extensively about healthy, productive ways to express your feelings and communicate your wants and needs.

Once again:
1. Become AWARE of what your depression is masking.
2. ACKNOWLEDGE it to yourself and to someone else. Express it constructively. A few well-chosen screams on the freeway won't hurt you or the person they're aimed at. "Step on a crack, break your mother's back." Remember that? How guilty I felt as I stomped on every crack I could find when I was angry at Mom and too afraid to tell her!
3. ACCEPT your anger, fear, or whatever other underlying feelings you have. You are human; therefore, you will have the entire gamut of human feelings, whether you think they're acceptable or not.

As you incorporate the three A's into your life, the Masks of Fear will gradually drop away.

*"Woman is buffeted by circumstances so long as
she believes herself to be
the creature of outside conditions,
but when she realizes that
she is a creative power,
and that she may command
the hidden soil and seeds
of her being out of which circumstances grow,
she then becomes the rightful master of herself."*

—Transcribed by DOROTHY J. HULST

CHAPTER 4

Natural And Learned Fears

Natural Fears

A baby is born with only two natural fears: the fear of falling and fear of loud noises. When a baby is about to fall, or hears a loud noise, it goes immediately into a fear response, inhaling sharply and stiffening. The initial physical response is followed by panicked crying. As adults, we still experience these primal, natural fears. *All* other fears, including fear of death, are learned.

We are naturally curious but *not* naturally fearful.

Learned Fears

Our culture, our families, and our governments use fear to control us. Fear can be a useful and beneficial means of instruction, but too often it's applied inappropriately, and we're conditioned to unhealthy fearfulness. We come out of childhood wearing the yoke of our family and society's unresolved fears. In time we make them our own.

> *How does fear, or other emotion come about? We humans tend to believe that fear is created by the approach of the fearsome thing—the snake creeping towards us. But actually the small child tends to be curious rather than frightened by such things, until conditioned by the mother's gasp and frantic reaction. Thereafter the emotion of fear arises in the child when a snake approaches. But it is not created by the snake. It is created by the connection made in our mind. It is caused by what we tell ourselves about snakes.*
>
> —Elizabeth Gawain

My mother was deathly afraid of dogs. She never taught me to fear dogs, but as a child my sensitive mind registered her fear response whenever a dog appeared. I learned "Dogs are dangerous." Even though I've never been bitten and have known only one person who was bitten, my body reacts with a fear-response whenever I see a strange dog.

> *Fear is created not by the world around us, but in the mind, by what we think is going to happen.*
>
> —Elizabeth Gawain

Of course, fear may also be learned as a result of traumatic experiences. If some fearful thing has happened to you, you may need the help of a minister, therapist, or other professional to help you uncover and heal your inner wounds.

The good news about learned fear is that it can be *unlearned*. Unlearning fear takes a strong desire to be free, a willingness to work to retrain yourself, and *patience*. In our era of supersonic flights, split-second computers, and fast food, we have come to expect instant gratification. Don't expect to be served up a fear-free life just by reading this book, as you would expect to get french fries from McDonald's. Self-discovery, growth, and change do not work that way. Yes, there will be sudden, breathtaking insights, but without patient work and commitment to a day-to-day process of change, they will quickly fade.

I have been working for 20 years now to remove my tenacious fear of rejection. When I first began, patience was by no means my strong suit, and there were times when I felt discouraged to the point of despair. Sometimes I backslid or crept forward slowly, but I can truly say that now my fear of rejection is only a bare thread, a fragile web limiting my life, whereas when first discovered, it was a heavy chain and anchor.

We *can* relearn our fundamental attitudes toward life and experience the deep truth that our lives and relationships need *not* be fear-filled. We are not our fear; we merely experience it. Thus we can gradually learn to see fear not as something that we *are* but something that we *have*. For example, you may at times have told yourself, "I'm such a coward!" Not true! Never accept a definition of yourself as identified with your fear. You may feel fearful, but that doesn't mean you're a coward. Any committed attempt you make to disidentify yourself from your fears deserves to be called brave, even heroic. And you *can* learn to disidentify from your fears.

Gradually, you will learn to see yourself as larger and stronger than your fears. As you begin to disidentify with paralyzing fear, you'll begin to have more control over your life. Here's an exercise in disidentification: the next time you're AWARE of fear, ACKNOWLEDGE what you're feeling, ACCEPT that it's a fact of your being at the moment, and then repeat several times to yourself: "I have a fear of (heights, failure, oysters, etc.), but *I* am not this fear!"

We have come to believe that we *are* what we feel. Not so! Feelings are absolutely important, but they aren't the totality of who we are. We are much, much more than our feelings. You might try this further exercise: think of some sentences that appeal to you as accurate definitions of who you are—for example:

> I am a child of God.
> I am a pure center of self-consciousness.
> I am.
> I am perfect.
> I am too amazing to fathom.

Then, choose the sentence that is most powerful to you, and add it to the foregoing affirmation of disidentification. I might say: *I have a fear of rejection, but*

I am not this fear. I am a beautiful, unique soul created in God's image.

Use whatever works for *you*. It will work powerfully to keep you from being sucked into the vortex of your fear.

Buried Fears

We can't always be protected as we're growing up, so it's inevitable that we'll have experiences which range from a bit scary to completely terrifying. When something happens to us as small children, we often have no way to verbalize our feelings and thereby let others know that we need help and healing. Children who can communicate their feelings, whether through bad behavior or a good, healthy scream, are the lucky ones. Less fortunate are those children who repress frightening incidents, shutting them away from conscious awareness.

Children often feel responsible for the events that happen in their lives. If a parent dies, or if parents argue, it must be the child's fault. The child's developing ego structure is not yet able to perceive cause and effect as pertaining to others. The child sees itself as the center of its universe, the pivotal point around which all events revolve, therefore it assumes responsibility for whatever takes place. Thus, children who repress their fears usually end up feeling not only fearful, but bad and unworthy as well.

The story of Victoria is a good case in point. As an adult, Victoria appeared to be well-adjusted and successful. She had a good education, a fulfilling job, children, and a supportive husband. She came from an apparently loving, though straightlaced and repressive family. When she entered therapy, she was suffering from continuous nightmares, a crushing fear of going to bed alone, chronically low self-esteem, and acute suicidal tendencies. She felt crazy, and the question "Why?" haunted her.

Victoria blamed herself for not snapping out of her depression. After losing an alarming amount of weight and thinking constantly of suicide, she sought therapy. With support from her husband, and from me as her therapist, and with tremendous courage on her part, she allowed a series of long-buried memories to rise to conscious awareness.

Beginning in infancy, Victoria had been repeatedly sexually molested, and physically threatened. Because her fear was so great and her sense of shame and guilt so powerful, she had repressed all conscious awareness of these atrocities. Not until she was 36 years old and faced with overwhelming personal crises did her defenses begin to crumble.

Painful as Victoria's memories were, it was extremely important that they emerge from hiding, from the dungeons where she'd kept them locked away. Now there was a *known* reason for her seemingly groundless fears. She was *not* crazy, as she had thought. The fears she'd experienced were entirely appropriate, considering what she had endured as a child. Now healing could begin.

Our fears are clues that there are hidden things inside us which need healing.

As you can see from the extreme example of Victoria, unresolved fears can be debilitating, even life-threatening. Having the courage to search for the source of your fears is a necessary first step toward being who you really are, free from limitations and able to live your life to your fullest potential.

If you are experiencing fears that seem rootless, out of all proportion to the apparent cause, or have no "logical" basis, give yourself a priceless gift: explore them. Only when they're brought to conscious awareness will you be able to discover how to heal them. So long as they remain hidden, you'll have no choice in the matter—you'll be held helplessly in their grasp.

Most hidden fears are stashed away because at one time it seemed safer to hide them than be aware of them. When they emerge, you may feel the original fears all over again. Thus, it's essential to find a climate of safety in which to explore them. You must be able to have the conviction that the risk you're taking in exposing the origin of your fears is something that you can safely handle. Before you begin to explore, find a person or a group with whom you feel safe, people you can trust implicitly with your vulnerability.

Since the origin of our fears most often lies in childhood, we can expect to experience childlike fear while re-discovering them. Seeking emotional support at such times is not dependence; it is wisdom.

Emotional dependence means *having* to have others to survive, wanting others to "do it for us," depending on others to give us our self-image, make our decisions, and take care of us financially, for example. But there will be many times, while we learn to disidentify with our fears, when we'll need the support of others. Wouldn't you think it self-defeating if a friend was run over by a truck, but wouldn't allow doctors to set her broken bones, or friends to aid her in her convalescence?

Letting others nurture and support us at certain times helps us heal more quickly. When we're run over by an emotional truck, it is silly to think we "shouldn't burden other people." The facade of stiff-upper-lip encourages repression, not healing. Repression imprisons. Healing frees.

Fear Creates Reality and "Circumstances"

Our fears are like magnets that attract to us the things we fear the most. If our mind is tuned to an internal channel which consistently repeats fearful litanies, fear will be our experience. But we can change the channel! A helpful technique in this respect is to avoid negative statements that begin with "I am":

> *I am fearful.*
> *I am scared of authority.*
> *I am unemployable.*
> *I am a fraidy cat.*
> *I am a coward.*
> *I am ugly.*

Such statements are self-fulfilling. If we wear negative name tags, we'll attract negative "company." In this way our inner thoughts and feelings create our external circumstances.

Many martial arts instructors believe that attitude is just as important as the physical movements of their particular discipline. Thus, they concentrate on creating attitudes of confidence and safety in their students. Granted, it helps to know how to defend yourself physically from attack, but at least as important is releasing any "victim feelings" that you've been carrying.

Breaking out of a "victim" mode of thinking can be tough, and it usually helps a great deal to find a qualified instructor or therapist who can guide you. If you've been a victim of abuse, incest, rape, or some other form of violation, please seek professional help. The wounds caused by such traumatic experiences may be much deeper than you realize, and to heal them effectively requires expert guidance.

Instead of using "I am" statements when talking about your fears, say:

> *I have a fear of (rejection, etc.).*
> *I sometimes experience a fear of (authority).*
> *I can at times feel like a (coward).*
> *I have a fear of (failure/success).*
> *When I stand up in front of a group, I feel*
> *(nervous, tongue-tied, dumb).*

With such statements, you acknowledge that you have fears, but you don't identify yourself as *being* them. The difference is subtle, but important: you *have* fears, and you can *heal* them. You are *not* your fears.

As you learn to heal your fears, you'll learn also to act without letting them limit you. Nowadays, whenever I notice a fear crying out in my body, I say: "Thanks, Body, I hear you." Then I check it out to see if the fear is valid now or an old response. If it is an old pattern, I say to it: "I'm going to go ahead and do what I need to do as if you weren't there."

Too often, a wrong interpretation of our fears prevents us from acting. We believe we shouldn't be feeling fear, and so we try waiting until we feel perfectly at ease in order to tackle the difficulty that lies before us. This strategy never works. Many of our accomplishments happen in spite of fear. In fact, in many instances, anxiety and fear can actually propel us into action.

Bill Russell of the Boston Celtics, one of the all-time greats of pro basketball, would get so nervous before each game that he'd vomit, yet he never let his fear keep him from being a world-class player. There's something especially heroic about his having used his talent to the utmost despite his fears.

One of my hobbies is acting. I love auditioning, and I thrive on rehearsals because creating a character is such a thrill for me. *But!!* The first night in front of an audience is agony. I am *terrified*. I wonder why I ever decided to do something so ridiculous. Why have I set myself up to fail? Surely I'll make a complete fool of myself and let the cast down in the process. All of my lines vanish from my memory. In short, I have a colossal case of stage fright.

To a lesser degree, the same thing happens each time I stand up in front of a group to lead a seminar or give a talk. But I do it anyway. Once I get into the swing of it, I have a great time. It's almost as if the energy generated by my fear propels me into doing a better job.

This process can backfire, as it did for me on one memorable occasion. It happened at a high school "Lit Night" where all of the literary clubs competed in speeches, monologues,. and poetry readings. I was to do a funny monologue about girdles (remember those?). The girl who went on before me forgot her lines, and my reaction was cold-footed terror that I'd do it too. Sure enough, though I knew my lines cold, I had tuned my mind to a panic channel, and my fearful inner dialogue resulted in an actual loss of memory.

I am learning not to let fear keep me from doing what I want to do. It isn't fun to suffer stage fright—I'm not exactly crazy about perspiring down to my waistband and feeling nauseated and panicky. But I've learned through experience that when I face this fear and move through it, it diminishes, and I end up enjoying the very activities that activated the fear in the first place.

Taking small steps despite fear is called "desensitization." As we persevere and *do*, in spite of fear, fear begins to lose its grip on us.

Robin, a client of mine, was afraid to drive out of town. We began to desensitize her by having her (in the safety of my office) close her eyes and imagine herself driving. When anxiety arose, we used relaxation techniques. When she could visualize herself on the freeway and driving away from home without anxiety, she took another small step: while sitting in the driveway in her car, she visualized herself driving out of town. When she felt able to move on to a further small step, she drove about a mile from home. With small, successful steps, she mastered her fear and now feels fine driving almost anywhere.

Remember, this statement from the Bible expresses a deep truth: "Lo, the thing I feared the most has come to pass." If we fear illness, we are likely to become ill. If we fear abandonment and rejection, we will inevitably experience them in our lives. Speaking for myself, when I fear rejection, I approach people guardedly, making people feel that

I'm cool, or that I don't trust them. Thus my fear causes the very rejection that I'm trying so hard to protect myself against.

Many of us, unfortunately, have a lifelong legacy of fear. The task before us is to outgrow that limiting inheritance and claim our true birthright: the freedom and courage to be ourselves.

In Chapter 14, I'll give you practical methods for transforming the negative magnetism of your fears. But you can begin immediately to change your thoughts. No matter how many times fear attacks you, keep affirming that those fears are not you, and that someday you will completely overcome them. Gradually, day by day, your positive affirmations will grow in strength until they begin to push back those old barriers of fear. Remember: your fears are not you, and you are not them. You can diminish them. You can act in spite of them. You can be free.

Review your past in an atmosphere of healing gentleness and self-respect. You've already done a lot of courageous work—you've survived despite obstacles. Give yourself credit for your inborn heroism, and keep working to realize your birthright of freedom.

The first problem for all of us, men and women, is not to learn, but to unlearn.

—GLORIA STEINEM

CHAPTER 5

*Underlying Assumptions
And Hidden Beliefs:
Things We've Swallowed
Whole*

IN THIS CHAPTER I'll explore some of our unconscious beliefs and assumptions—how we got them, why we're afraid to look at our hidden dragons, and what we can do about them when we do see them.

As we grow up, we are exposed to many attitudes, ideas, feelings, and prejudices held by our parents, families, and the society at large. We absorb and mimic what we see and feel around us.

We are constantly inundated by stimuli, subliminal messages, and suggestions, many of which are detrimental to our inner growth and freedom:

> *"You aren't the only pebble on the beach!"*
> *"If you can't say anything nice, don't say
>   anything at all."*
> *"You'll never be hung for your beauty."*

These statements come from the book *Momalies: as Mother Used to Say*. We all grow up hearing similar things, which were limiting because as children, we *believed* them. We swallowed them whole. In my opinion, that book would be better entitled *Momma Lies*.

Why wouldn't we believe such statements? After all, children have little discernment and depend entirely on their parents, teachers, and other adults to teach them the truth about life. As we grow older, we receive further instruction:

> *"Women should be kept barefoot and pregnant."*
> *"A woman's place is in the home."*
> *"Physical beauty is essential for happiness."*
> *(And more subtly) "Men are more valuable than women."*

The messages we swallow whole as children become our own underlying assumptions and implicit beliefs, and we guide our lives accordingly. Because most of these notions are hidden, we're unaware of the extent to which they rule our actions and reactions—unless we ferret them out consciously in order to transform them. "Underlying" is the appropriate word, since they are *under* our conscious awareness, and *lie* to us about reality.

Our assumptions govern us much as an automatic pilot guides an airplane. For example, if we have hidden beliefs that life is hard or sex is dirty, we will have feelings which correspond to those beliefs. Thus, beliefs hidden from conscious awareness may emerge as unconsciously motivated actions. In fact, our actions will reflect our hidden feelings.

On the occasion of Jane's engagement, her father

gave her the only heart-to-heart talk they'd ever had. He thought she should be told that her mother was frigid and that the possibility existed that she might be, herself.

Until then she had enjoyed sex, although she had felt a little guilty about her pleasure. Jane had been told all her life that she was just like her mother; thus the horrible thought entered her mind that she might also be frigid. She immediately tried to hide the thought from herself, but sex began to be a problem for her and her new husband. Only when her underlying assumptions and fears were brought to the surface, acknowledged, and accepted did she discover that she was in fact a healthy, sensual, and sexual woman. Dad had dished out the possibility of frigidity, and she had swallowed it whole.

Our unconscious assumptions create attitudes and actions that influence our lives in ways of which we may be completely unaware. They often shape our choice of husband, career, home, friends, and lifestyle.

Mary became aware that for years she had consistently been choosing men who were less intelligent than she, usually men whom she could dominate. Her relationships were often painful and caused her to experience a frustrating intellectual isolation.

Mary's father, who was mentally unbalanced, dominated her mother totally. Her mother's fear of "upsetting" him kept her in the position of a victim. Even as a young girl, Mary was aware of her mother's shame and rage at the imbalance in the relationship. Mary had felt her mother's pain, concluded that relationships were all one-sided, and vowed that she would never be the inferior partner.

Although she had hidden this awareness from herself, she acted it out in her adult relationships by choosing men whom she could dominate. Until she discovered the underlying beliefs that were guiding her actions, Mary hadn't considered the possibility that she might live side by side with someone as an equal partner.

Uncovering hidden beliefs and underlying assumptions opens crucial doors to personal growth.

How many times have you heard women say, "I just can't do (_____) or (_____)!" Here's an example of a widely-held underlying assumption: "Women aren't as good in math as men are." Studies of young children have shown that girls are naturally just as adept in math as boys are. However, as girls grow up and are subjected to subtle (and not so subtle) messages from teachers, parents, peers, and prejudiced literature, they believe the lie: they begin to live "down" to others' expectations.

In grade school and early high school, I made all A's in math and received the highest grade in my sophomore class on a standardized geometry test. Sometime after my sophomore year, though, I began to buy into the popular belief that girls can't do math. Today, I feel dazed by a bank statement. I can hear myself thinking, "I *can't* do this." And, consequently, I can't. Because math isn't a necessary part of my professional or personal life, I haven't tried too hard to overcome that particular assumption. If it becomes necessary, I will, in the full awareness of its origins. (For now, I just plain don't wanna concentrate on math!)

As we uncover hidden beliefs that limit us and replace them with valid assumptions and beliefs, we take a giant step forward in changing our behavior, our feelings, our lives. By healing false assumptions and attitudes, we create whole new patterns of behavior for ourselves and for others in our lives. Every time we break a new path in "inner healing travel," we make it a bit easier for others to travel into and heal their own wounded inner regions.

Beliefs

Each of us functions inside a set of beliefs. In our lives, belief systems create order and structure. They make important decisions easier to make, and they provide the basis for our ethics, morality, and philosophy. Our personalities are structured by the beliefs we learned from parents, teachers, friends, and the culture around us.

Our parents' beliefs have become our own. As adults we no longer need to be told right from wrong because our parents' voices are implanted within us, telling us how to behave and what's expected of us.

Our beliefs also arise from the ways we *interpret* what we see and hear as we grow up. And it's interesting to note that our beliefs frequently are based far more on interpretation than on fact. Mildred always cut the end off the ham before baking it. She never questioned the correctness of that behavior until her son asked her about it one day. She did it because her mother did it. When he probed further, her son discovered that his grandmother had a very logical explanation for cutting off the end of the ham: her baking pan was too small to accommodate a whole ham. Mildred's belief was based not on a

universal truth but on her own, unthinking interpretation of her mother's actions as right and
proper, whatever their origin.

Our belief systems can also be created from fear.
If we fear rejection, we may believe that it isn't safe
to disagree with others. When our views run con-
trary to popular opinion, we may find it hard to
speak our minds. Why? Because we fear we'll be
rejected.

The culture around us propagates erroneous beliefs, too, such as: "Men are more powerful than
women," and "Men should make more money because they have families to support." (Actually, one
of every three families in America today is wholly
supported by a woman.)

We give lip service to the idea that a woman's
work in the home is as important as a man's work—
until it comes to assigning a dollar value to the work
performed. Women too easily acquiesce to the prev-
alent belief that the money her husband brings
home is his to mete out as he sees fit. The belief that
we have no money of our own can keep us feeling
dependent on the men in our lives, confused about
our rights, and limited in our choices. A woman
who believes this way will feel unable to stop destructive behavior in the home, including physical
and emotional abuse.

Although we need beliefs to guide us, false beliefs bind us to limitation. One form of false belief is
unquestioned assumptions about other women:

> *"Women are over-emotional."*
> *"Women are catty and petty."*
> *"Women can't be trusted."*
> *"Women aren't as capable as men."*

When my first husband left me for my "good friend," I began to believe that "women can't be trusted." Yet, with that one painful exception, and a few excruciating high-school traumas, that hadn't been my experience of women. I now *felt* I couldn't trust them, yet my life was virtually filled with trustworthy women. My new belief was creating paradoxes in my life, and since the rational mind has difficulty living with paradoxes, I buried the conflict away in my subconscious—thereby creating some pretty irrational feelings toward my loyal friends. Fortunately, the origins of my feelings of distrust began to dawn on me, and I was able to talk to my friends and free myself from the inner turmoil.

A most important part of your work toward growth and change will come from examining your belief systems regarding all areas of life. Especially important are your beliefs about other women, because negative beliefs about your women friends will separate you from *the very people who can share and empathize with you in your struggle.* When you isolate yourself from other women, you are subtly isolating yourself from yourself.

To gain the courage to be yourself, you need to deal with beliefs that are keeping you stuck. What beliefs have you swallowed whole, that you now find aren't working for you? What beliefs, assumptions, and attitudes are you holding onto even though they no longer enhance your life? It is time to free yourself from worn-out beliefs.

Though it's often hard for us to give up the old habit of asking, "Mother, may I? (or Father, or Husband)," we're living in an age when we have unprecedented opportunities to make our own decisions—to be ourselves. As we unravel our emotional dependencies, we learn that no one can fill us with confidence, independence, and a sense of inner worth but ourselves, with the help of whatever we interpret as a higher Power, Energy, or God.

People, being only human, are bound to let us down. We often long to return to the easy fantasy that it's okay to be emotionally dependent, that our men will take care of us, that it's *their* responsibility to keep us safe and support us. To *really know* that the buck stops with ourselves is frightening, but it's also extremely freeing to realize that we can be independent, confident, and in control of ourselves. We are all—men and women—called to *grow up*, to assume responsibility for ourselves. As grownups we are better able to love independently, interdependently, and joyfully.

Seed Sentences: Weeds or Flowers?

Seed sentences are clusters of ideas, words, or scripts that we all create in order to keep us congruent with our underlying assumptions and hidden beliefs.

Most seed sentences remain unspoken, perhaps even subconscious. They are bits and pieces of ideas we've picked up along the way; now, they form the heart of our beliefs about ourselves.

Seed sentences come from many sources: parents, TV, movies, magazines, advertising—yet they contribute to our images of how we're supposed to live and what we expect to receive from life and from others. Our lives, in effect, sprout from these seed sentences we carry within.

If all of our seed sentences blossomed into flowers, our lives would be gardens filled with beauty and grace. In fact, most of us have picked up weed seeds that grow into thistles and thorns, choking our creativity and the realization of our authentic selves.

Some examples of *flower* seed sentences:

> *"I am a worthwhile person."*
> *"I deserve to be loved."*
> *"I am lovable."*
> *"I can do anything I set my mind to."*

If seed sentences such as these are germinating in your subconscious, you will probably have a wonderful life, filled with loving relationships. When you look in the mirror in the morning, you are happy with what you see.

Weed sentences might sound something like this:

> *"I can never do anything right."*
> *"I don't deserve to be loved."*
> *"I'm no good at (_____) or*
> *(_____)."*
> *"Everyone handles things better than I do."*

If you're carrying around weed sentences, you undoubtedly feel pretty down on yourself. When people try to love you, you question their motives. "How can they love *me*? They must not be very bright." Weed sentences go hand in hand with low self-esteem.

Brenda, a high school senior, felt that she was a

loser. Her seed sentences were: "I'm too fat. Thunder Thighs is my name. I'm too stupid." (She had an A-minus average.) "I'm not attractive to boys. I've never been kissed!"

With these weed sentences buzzing in her head, she had developed a caustic exterior that scared people away. Whenever she had a crush on a boy, and he ventured to look past her tough facade, she began to consider him a geek. Anyone interested in her was surely a loser. This double bind kept her from having what she wanted.

In therapy, we began to pull some of her weed sentences and replace them with lovely flower seed sentences. Eventually, she went off to college, leaving not one but two very nice young men sorry to see her go.

Another example of the power of seed sentences is Connie. On the afternoon when she received her master's degree, Connie remembered her first grade teacher saying to her mother, "It's nice that Connie is pretty, because she's not very bright." She took that to heart, and no matter how good her grades were in school, she felt dumb. Her teacher's comment had become an internalized seed sentence: "I'm pretty, but I'm dumb." Quite a weed!

How do we pick up our packet of thought-seeds? People make the most unbelievably careless statements within the sensitive hearing of children: "She has a face only a mother can love." "You're about as graceful as a bull in a china shop." Children take such pronouncements as authoritative because they come from people who are ten feet tall.

"But I was only teasing . . ." Ever hear that one? It didn't make you feel any better, did it? Teasing is veiled hostility and is almost never funny, unless the teasee has openly agreed to relate that way. There is gentle, loving teasing, but 98% of the time (I just made up that figure), teasing is hurtful.

No matter how old we are, we all have sensitive areas through which insidious sentences can penetrate to our subconscious minds. We all feel especially vulnerable to certain types of suggestion. For example, I once discovered a seed sentence I'd been carrying around since childhood: "Women are not happy." No one had told me that, but as a little girl I *felt* it was true. The women I knew certainly didn't seem very happy: they sighed and complained a lot. As I grew up, I collected data that supported my underlying belief that women aren't happy. One of my mother's favorite laments, uttered with a sigh or from between clenched teeth, was: "A man may work from sun to sun, but a woman's work is never done." I asked myself, "How can women be happy if they have to work all the time?" My inner computer plunked another byte for unhappiness.

Perhaps predictably, my first marriage was unhappy, and only gradually did I realize that my unhappiness had preceded my marriage. Strange as it may sound, I was uncomfortable when I felt happy. Whenever I became happy, I'd get scared because I felt somehow off-balance, so I'd pick a fight, become moody, or sabotage a pleasant situation. Unhappiness was my unconscious comfort zone. Being unhappy kept me congruent with my underlying belief that women are not happy.

I began to be aware of my self-defeating underlying belief, and I began to work to change it. Bit by bit, I gave myself permission to be happy. Every time I spotted the old pattern of happiness-sabotage, I stopped and reassured myself that it was okay to feel this good. I replaced my weed senten-ces with: "I have the right to be happy. It is okay to feel great!" I'm now very comfortable with happi-ness, and I've invented some new seed sentences to affirm this new awareness: "Women deserve to be happy *and* have fun! *I* deserve to be happy and have fun!"

We always gravitate toward the familiar and shun the unknown. When we go against our seed senten-ces, we feel a loss of our integrity. We don't trust what is outside of our experience. My experience had been that women weren't happy. That doesn't mean it was even true of the grownups I observed, only that I perceived it as being true.

In the midst of a pleasant afternoon with her brother and his family, Lily found herself becoming depressed for no apparent reason. As she traced the thread of her thoughts, she discovered a seed sen-tence working in the background: "All good things must come to an end." She had begun to grieve over their departure hours before they were to leave. Her seed sentence was conditioning her to be wary of loss. She couldn't enjoy the moment because of its foreshadowed ending.

"If I'm rejected, I'll die." Such internalized seed sentences sound dramatic and grandiose; but the not-okay child in us in fact perceives rejection as life-threatening. When we become aware of such debilitating seed sentences, we can start the process of replacing them with opposite, healing thoughts. With our new awareness of the inner terror of life-threatening rejection, we are free to choose thoughts that help us become consciously self-directed, rather than controlled by hidden assump-tions and beliefs.

Many of our semi-conscious seed sentences express fear of offending others. The trouble is, our freedom diminishes if we are afraid of standing up to others. I don't mean that I advocate unkindness or discourtesy—it's very important for our own self-esteem that we learn to think empathetically of others. But craving others' approval in order to feel okay about ourselves kills creativity and authenticity.

We shackle ourselves to others' moods. What happens when your husband, boss, or kids are in a lousy mood and nothing pleases them? Do you dance around like a trained bear, trying to make them laugh and be happy? I used to do that because I always felt that I was somehow to blame for other people's bad moods. When they were rejecting, I felt like less of a person. Their rejection was unbearable, and so I tried to dance to whatever tune they were inaudibly playing. It never worked, and I became increasingly angry with myself for behaving like a door mat.

I've learned that, to paraphrase the words of an excellent book by Laura Huxley, "I am not the target." I've learned how to step back from the situation. In the presence of angry or rejecting vibrations, my stomach still knots up, my throat closes, and I want to run to the nearest cookie jar for solace, but I say to my body and my internal little girl: "We're okay! We *are* safe!" With reassurance from these powerful new seed sentences, I find my scared feelings dissipating, and I end up feeling very pleased with myself. A threatening situation transformed into a pleasant inner victory, another bout of fear positively overcome without falling into the trap of emotional dependence: "Oh my God, I'll die if he/she/they don't love me *now!*"

At the end of this section you'll find a list of common seed sentences and nicknames that become seed sentences. What seed sentences did you gather as you grew up? List them in the space provided. Look at your seed sentences and begin to negate their power with your awareness. As you replace weed sentences with truth, you'll be freed from their stranglehold on your behavior. Name your seed sentences: roses, lilies, jonquils? Or pyracantha, poison ivy, stinkweed?

You can pull up your weed thoughts and replace them with "thought flowers" that will blossom into a beautiful life. In Chapter 14 I'll suggest some how-tos to help you do this.

WEED SENTENCES:
THINGS WE'VE SWALLOWED WHOLE

1. I should have been a boy.

2. Tears are a form of self-pity.

3. Wear a girdle and keep your legs crossed . . . nice girls don't . . .

4. Nice girls do more than their share.

5. Women are not happy.

6. I am responsible for another person's happiness.

7. Women/men can't be trusted.

8. It's a cruel world out there.

9. Women over 40 aren't attractive.

10. I'm ugly, unlovable, (_____), or (_____).

11. I can't . . .

12. Don't air your dirty laundry.

13. I've always got to be "up."

14. Nothing I do is good enough.

15. That's men's work (or that's women's work).

16. The children are totally my responsibility.

17. My sister (lover, brother, father, dog) is better than I am.

18. Life is hard and then you die.

YOUR OWN WEED SENTENCES

1. _____
2. _____
3. _____
4. _____
5. _____
6. _____

NICKNAMES

1. Chubby Cheeks
2. Lardo
3. Fatty Patty
4. Stick
5. Freck
   (as in freckles)
6. Sappy Sue
7. Four Eyes
8. Thunder Thighs
9. Bucky
10. Baby
11. Rug Rat
12. Shnoz

SOME OF YOUR NICKNAMES

1. _____
2. _____
3. _____
4. _____

The Brothers Grim:
Religion and Society

Two of the most powerful forces that shape our beliefs are religion and society. In the past, women have rarely questioned the truth or reality of religious and societal assumptions. And they've felt powerless to change what they felt was erroneous.

One of our greatest foes has been our own internal sense of authority, which has kept us believing whatever our political, cultural, and religious institutions have told us about women. Until just a few years ago, men virtually owned "their" women. As soon as she married, a woman's property became her husband's. (This is still the case in many countries.) Fathers paid young men dowries to assume responsibility for their daughters. This practice may have made certain women feel materially secure, but it hardly encouraged young women to think of themselves as unique and valuable.

Have you ever secretly believed that society felt sorry for your father because you aren't a boy? Worse, have you ever thought your parents were disappointed that you were a girl? Many of us have picked up our society's passed-down belief that women are in various respects "less than" men.

While many of us can look back at our early religious affiliations feeling that they gave us security, love, and the encouragement to become our best selves, others weren't so fortunate. What we heard in church was: "Lord, forgive me a miserable sinner." In many religions, guilt and sin are bedrock concepts. All men (!) were born sinners, and if you sin you'll suffer anything from eternal roasting in a molten lake of fire to many lifetimes of atonement for the bad karma you've incurred.

The word "sin" is actually a term from archery which means "to miss the mark"—a far more kindly interpretation than it's given by many orthodox religions. In fact, few denominations are satisfied with the Bible's definitions of sin (in the Ten Commandments, say). The people in power in the churches feel duty bound to create new sins: not long ago a woman who showed her ankles was a Jezebel. A girl who smoked was a scarlet woman.

It pays to sort through the seed sentences you've carried over from your association with religion and society. A remarkable number of my clients come from backgrounds of guilt-fostering religious environments. Guilt and fear prevent them from experiencing their authentic selves.

Lynn is a successful businesswoman, a single mother, respected and loved in her community. She spent her childhood in a strict, church-run school where obeying the rules was the paramount requirement. She never disobeyed, but she also never felt okay about herself, no matter how much outward approval she won. In therapy she had a vivid, painful recollection of a severe teacher telling her, "You *never* get it right!" Lynn, a sensitive child, internalized that thought until it became a large belief system about herself, accompanied by the seed sentence: "I never do it right." As an adult, even though she often *did* do it right, she never *felt* like a person who could do it right.

I believe in spirituality, but I don't think we can experience our *authentic* spiritual selves until we have ferreted out the unquestioned, self-condemning beliefs we've acquired in our contact with some orthodox religions and society.

Faith in the Spirit within is every bit as important to us, in our search for the courage to be ourselves, as are physical health, emotional stability, and mental clarity. All the world's religions are united in saying that the spiritual life is, above all, a life of ever-expanding love, kindness, positive affirmation, and joy. In order to expand, you need to free yourself from the negativity and guilt-festering, sin-fostering consciousness of people whose vision falls far short of love.

Change takes time and doesn't come easily. As you work to bring your beliefs into harmony with the goal of loving support for yourself, a sense of humor will come in handy. A friend whom I admire very much says, "Get the giggle on it." Laughter—seeing things as really not all that serious—increases your courage to be yourself.

Become AWARE of your beliefs. Bring them into the light of your present, adult knowledge. ACKNOWLEDGE that they are what they are. Then ACCEPT that they are what you've believed until now. Finally, begin working patiently to change them.

*Our strength
is often composed of the weaknesses
we're damned if we're going to show.*

—MIGNON McLAUGHLIN

CHAPTER 6

Beyond Fear: Transforming The Dragons

HOW DO PARENTS ENCOURAGE the infant who's just learning to walk? They hold her hand, provide a safe environment, and congratulate each new success.

Similarly, in moving beyond fear, realize that you must go forward at a beginner's pace. Take baby steps. Be proud of each faltering toddle, each newly taken footstep. Become a kind and encouraging parent to yourself. Gently congratulate yourself on your successes, and comfort yourself after your failures.

Self-hate never does any good. How often have you said to yourself, "I just hate my fear of rejection." Or, "I just hate myself when I overeat." Did hating yourself ever decrease your fear of rejection (or your waistline) by a single millimeter? Take a second now to go back and read those two self-hating statements. Notice where the power lies: "I just hate my fear of rejection" translates to "I *am* afraid of rejection—I *affirm* it and hate it."

Self-hate drives its object even deeper into our consciousness. Why not try a little experiment: the next time you're tempted to feel self-hate, whether it's for "pigging out" before bedtime or letting someone dominate you, try the Love and Acceptance Cure. Who, exactly, is expecting you to hate yourself for what happened? Right: *no one!* Talk to yourself in a spirit of love and acceptance. Be on your own side. Sure, you could have done better, but what you need right now is a good friend—you!—to laugh gently and encourage you.

Talk to yourself. It's by no means crazy—we do it all the time anyway. But talk nicely! Would your house plants wither if you talked to them in the way you've been talking to yourself? Create an internal atmosphere of love and acceptance so you'll have the courage to become aware of your fears and feelings.

Negativity *never* heals negativity. As a wise person once said, "You can't get rid of the darkness by beating at it with a stick. You must turn on the light." Become AWARE of what's going on inside you. Remember, feelings are in themselves neither right nor wrong; they merely *are*. If you understand them and allow them to be, without judging them, they'll move on, heal, and become transmuted. If you fearfully resist them, labeling them bad/wrong/ugly, they'll stick to your mind and grow. ACKNOWLEDGE your feelings. You don't need to act on them; just *see* them. Then, ACCEPT them. A gentle climate of love and acceptance fosters healing and growth.

Steps Toward Transformation

AWARE	Become aware of your drag-ons and fears
ACKNOWLEDGE	Invite your dragons into the light (take a dragon to lunch)
ACCEPT	Feelings aren't right or wrong; they just *are*.

Change is action; old habits are reactions. To change, you must consciously choose new actions. All the buried patterns we've talked about so far are ingrained, passive, fixed, change-resisting *reactions* to people and circumstances. The only way to be free of them is to create fresh, new *actions* to replace them. We need to *act* rather than *react*.

The three stages we talked about earlier (Aware, Acknowledge, Accept) are the basic tools of change. Now let me share with you a somewhat wider perspective on self-change:

STEP 1	is the three A's: AWARE, ACKNOWL-EDGE, and ACCEPT.
STEP 2	is PAUSE. Wait before you act. Give yourself time to assess your feelings (Step 1). A deliberate Pause is especially effective during heated conversations. Examine your feelings—then compare your options: remember how you have reacted in the past. Is it

appropriate now, or would you rather choose deliberate, creative, healing actions?

STEP 3   is CHOOSE. This step is crucial! By pausing, you've taken yourself off "automatic pilot" so that you're no longer merely reacting to people, situations, or inner feelings. Now you are free to chart your course in whatever direction seems the best.

If you take a single word out of this book and make it your own on a day-to-day basis, I hope it's "Choose." If you can *choose* to act in a different way, even while feeling the old way, you'll find it tremendously liberating!

My husband and I were having a confrontation in which I felt judged and rejected. I recognized an old reaction-pattern, a three-phase dance I used to go into whenever I felt threatened: first I'd feel guilty and wrong for "making" him unhappy, so I'd become jovial and conciliatory in order to jolly him out of his mood. When that didn't work, I became the counselor-in-residence and (oh, so calmly) pointed out the errors of his ways, reasonably citing the various psychological bases of the misunderstanding. That *never* worked. No one, especially our mate, is ever very receptive to being "enlightened" about the reasons for his or her irrational behavior while they're in the midst of feeling hurt, angry, or frustrated.

When neither of those tactics worked, I became frustrated, lonely, and discouraged. I would withdraw into righteous anger and slog around in a cloud of resentment and disappointment. Obviously, my mood was *his* fault. Why couldn't *he* be different? I had fallen into my "victim" stance.

During this particular episode, before the familiar pattern got into full swing, I *paused* and asked myself some very important questions:

1. *Have these reactions worked in the past?*
2. *Do I feel better when I react in these ways?*
3. *Is our relationship better after I've gone through the old, familiar reactions?*

In each case, the answer was a resounding "No!" So the next question was obvious:

4. *Do I still* want *to react this way?*

Now, having paused and stepped back from my feelings, I could *choose* how I would act.

I decided to detach myself—to withdraw from the events that were taking place—not in anger, resentment, or with a feeling of rejection, but in order to let *him* take responsibility for dealing with his feelings. I stopped trying to *fix* him or the situation. A sure sign of emotional dependence is trying to make everything "all better" for others, as if we were entirely responsible for their feelings.

Rather than reacting in my usual way I shut myself up with my tape recorder and made some notes for this book and another one. Instead of trying to convince my husband to change, I changed. I stepped out of the victim role, the overly-responsible role, and the I-must-be-wrong emotionally dependent role, and took care of myself.

From the neck up, I was exhilarated by the change in my behavior, but my body continued to behave in the old way. My stomach churned and giant talons seized my throat. My body felt guilty, rejected, scared, and lonely all at the same time.

I talked to my body and to my scared inner child, telling them that they were safe. I encouraged myself to relax and kept assuring myself that I was safe, and that I no longer needed the old feelings to protect me. Very slowly, my body began to get the message. After a few hours, the exhilaration in my head percolated through my entire body, and I felt great!

I had taken charge of my reactions and had thereby turned an old dragon into a new and better way of being in relationship with my husband. It was a very freeing experience, and healing also for him, since the old pattern had always created resentment and hostility toward him. My new pattern of actions had left us both free of having to deal with that!

Learn to entice your personal fear-dragons out of their caves. When you can work up the courage to do that, you'll begin moving toward greater and greater emotional freedom. As your dragons come into the light of awareness, and as your willingness and ability to face and heal inner fears increases, you'll be able to replace old dragons with new patterns, and you'll have wonderful experiences of new inner freedom.

Understanding and Transforming

STEP 1   . . . BECOME AWARE, ACKNOWLEDGE, AND ACCEPT.
Bring into the open old patterns, reactions, or fears.

STEP 2   . . . PAUSE
              Before you act, step back, take time
              out—a "breather"—to gain perspective.
              You can't see much with your nose
              pressed right up against what you're
              looking at.

STEP 3   . . . CHOOSE
              Decide on a course of action. How
              would you *like* to act? If the old reaction
              isn't working, *choose* to act in a new
              way. You *don't* have to continue old pat-
              terns. You are now in the driver's seat.

Learn to tolerate your fear-dragons without letting them carry you away. Take baby steps toward
risk. Ration your fear.

It also helps to have an emotional lifeline that's attached to a strong and steady tree. At various stages
in my life, those lifelines have been attached to my
mother, husband, children, therapist, friends, and
God.

> *Ration your fear*
> *Give it credence for awhile . . .*
> *Jumping off the high dive,*
> *You expect to be under water for a bit.*
> *The farther you fall, the longer it*
> *takes to break the surface.*
> *But surface you must,*
> *Or you will drown.*
> *Ration your fear.*
>
> —Moi'

Part Three

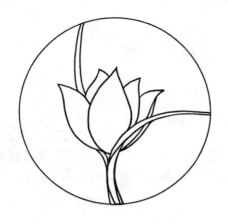

Unresolved Grief: Drowning In Life's Debris

Grief is a process.
If it is allowed,
healing will take place naturally.

—HOSPICE OF THE FOOTHILLS

Unresolved Grief: Drowning In Life's Debris

ALL OF US experience grief. We have small losses: rain on a vacation, gaining 10 pounds; and large losses: the loss of a job, illness, the death of a child.

A recent study measured the chemicals in tears. Those shed in happiness, awe, or other positive emotions were toxin-free, while tears shed in frustration, anger, fear, or grief had a significant poison-content.

Tears cleanse and heal. We need to weep over the discrepancies in our lives—the difference between our dreams and reality. All of us feel our losses and disappointments, but few of us feel free to grieve fully. A chasm of unresolved grief lies festering in our hearts.

Our local Hospice chapter has bereavement groups, which I lead. The people in these groups have all lost a person close to them. Some join the group while the loss is still very fresh in their minds and hearts. Naturally, their feelings are raw and excruciating. Many cry—and most apologize for doing so. Yet what could be more natural or healing than to weep for a grievous loss?

In our society, we feel we need to apologize for our tears, even for our feelings. There is good reason for this. Until recently neither society nor friends encouraged us to express feelings of grief. How many times have you heard someone say, "John is taking the death of his son so well." What that probably means is that John has suppressed his feelings and isn't acting out his suffering in front of others. As a society of "fixers," we are uncomfortable with another's un-fixable pain.

We resolve our discomfort by simply avoiding people who are experiencing pain. People who've gone through a divorce frequently tell me, "So many of my friends avoid me now." It's not that divorce renders you socially unacceptable; it's that friends can't "fix" it and don't know how to deal with the pain of the parties concerned, or with what it stirs up in themselves.

We're encouraged to let our grief sit, silent and unresolved, in the pit of our soul, where it becomes part of the dragged-around debris of our life. The *American Heritage Dictionary* defines "debris" as ". . . the scattered remains of something broken or destroyed; ruins, rubble, fragments . . ." I call it: "leftover stuff, unfinished business, old feelings that have never been healed."

Grief comes in many forms. Grief over death and

loss is just one form. Another is grief over the things we feel we should have done or shouldn't have done. When we fight with friends or mates, we grieve. When too many bills pile up and money is tight, we grieve. Anything unfinished and left to fester becomes emotional debris, the litter of unresolved grief. Debris is a mountain of garbage that stands in the path of our lives.

How can we collect that which is "scattered or broken" in our lives? Imagine a home in which no one ever swept up the fragments of broken dishes, no one ever took out the garbage, or used the disposal. In a very short while, that house would be uninhabitable. No one could live like that! (Except my son and daughter, when they were teenagers.)

The point is, many of us allow emotional debris to collect in our hearts, minds, and souls. Soon the mounds of dirt that we've swept under our emotional carpets become too big to ignore. They keep us from walking around freely in our own inner homes and separate us from those we care about. Those mounds of hidden debris soon erode our freedom to make conscious choices regarding how we will feel and act.

Loneliness
and the feeling of being unwanted
is the most terrible poverty.

—MOTHER TERESA

CHAPTER 7

Debris

Guilt

WOMEN FEEL GUILTY IF THEY:

DO	DON'T
Work	Work
Discipline the children	Discipline the children
Make more money than their husbands or fathers	Bring in "their share"
Take time for personal interests	Take time for personal interests
Get divorced	Have a happy marriage
Want free time and/or solitude	Nurture the spiritual side of their nature
Chat on the phone	Keep up their friendships
Say no	Say no
Have sex or want it	Have sex or want it
Get sick	Keep their bodies young and fit
Get angry	Stand up for themselves
Have children	Have children

Do you see yourself on that list? I do! I used to feel guilty if the cat had mats in its fur. Who said it was my responsibility to de-mat the cat? I did!

One of the biggest mounds swept under our emotional carpets is guilt. Among women, guilt spreads with the rampant fury of Bubonic plague. We feel guilty if our kids don't turn out as we think they should, as our parents think they should, or as society thinks they should. I know a woman whose son was an all-around superstar in high school. In college he burned out and left school. He didn't work much, and when he did, it was always in menial jobs. Her cry: "Where did I go wrong?"

We've been led to believe that we're responsible for others' happiness, success, moods, arguments, and failures. When our families aren't happy, it's *our* fault.

According to Lynne Caine, author of *What Did I Do Wrong? Mothers, Children, Guilt,* Sigmund Freud helped perpetuate this belief. In an interview, she said:

> *Our society is saturated with mother-blaming. This began, I believe, in the 1940s. That's when the popularizers of Freudian psychology discovered mothers were to blame for everything that went wrong with the American family. In 1942 Philip Wylie wrote* Generation of Vipers, *in which he proclaimed that Mom was a jerk. He coined the term "momism." From then on it's been open season on mothers. Mother-blaming—and in some cases mother-hating—abounds in our literature, movies, and TV. Mothers are portrayed as*

being either manipulative, possessive, controlling and bitchy, or as being wimpy, ineffectual and ludicrous.

This idea has become part of our belief system. For most of us, it's an underlying assumption—something we've swallowed whole. We create "Momist" seed sentences such as: "If my child, husband, or friend isn't happy, it's my fault." "I need to fix my husband's life." "I'm responsible for my child's successes in college."

Exaggerated affirmations of "responsibility" like these are loaded with guilt-producing power. In fact, we can never *make* people happy or successful; by feeling that we *must* make people happy, we merely set ourselves up for inevitable disappointments.

Years ago, my husband and I took a magazine quiz to see if we were compatible. One of the questions was: "When you and your spouse argue, is it sometimes/usually/always his/her fault?" My answer was "sometimes," and his was "always." He believed the myth that I was responsible for his happiness. Arguing made him unhappy, therefore if we argued, it must be my fault.

When we assume responsibility for another person's happiness, we set ourselves up to fail. I call it being a responsibility sponge. We become everybody's designated garbage can with a sign on us that tells our mates, children, parents and employers: "Dump here."

There was a time when, if there was a puddle of unhappiness around one of my kids or my husband, I was quick to leap in and try to mop it up. Having had two husbands and four kids, my sponge became extremely soggy! I believed that somehow I had failed them or offended them if they were unhappy, that it was part of my job as wife, mother, and human being never to offend anybody. But I discovered that *our freedom diminishes if we are afraid of standing up to others.*

I truly believed it was my role to carry everyone's garbage and mop up all puddles. If I didn't, I felt guilty. If I did and they didn't "get happy," I felt guilty *and* resentful. The role of responsibility sponge carries with it the need to teach others what they don't know, especially about feelings. As a therapist, I was especially subject to that delusion. I knew all about feelings. But my husband hated my preaching to him; it felt like I was playing combined roles of mother and teacher. Plays havoc with your love life!

While we do need loving relationships, we never need to turn our lives over to someone else or to take over responsibility for another person's life. By putting our happiness in others' hands, we become dependent; by taking responsibility for others' happiness, we invite them to become dependent—an invitation that the truly healthy human spirit always vigorously refuses.

Guilt is either appropriate or inappropriate. Appropriate guilt is a compass that tells you when you're going in the wrong direction. Like a sign, it looms on the road ahead, saying, "Stop. Wrong way." It's there to help; acknowledge it, and it subsides, its job done.

Naturally, there's appropriate guilt that's deep, long-lasting, and unusually painful. That kind of intensive, appropriate guilt signals a severe deviation from right behavior and the need for a very radical examination of your life. A murderer, or a child-abuser would hopefully sooner or later feel that kind of remorse.

Inappropriate guilt hangs on forever, paralyzing you with "if-only's" and "what-if's." A friend told me, "I have a round-trip ticket on the Guilt Train. Anytime it rolls through the station, I climb aboard!" Another friend who was with us quipped, "I never get off—station or not!"

WHERE DO WE GET ON THE GUILT TRAIN?

Children . . . little girls especially . . . are keenly tuned to the emotional vibrations of their parents and other adults. Children are exquisitely sensitive barometers for family feeling. From birth to the age of six or seven, children are not merely sensitive but also very self-centered. A five-year old is incapable of understanding outside causes; thus, whenever something happens in the home, in her mind, *she* caused it. If Mommy and Daddy fight, it's *her* fault.

As a little girl, I wore French braids. Every morning as my mother did my hair, she sighed repeatedly. Times were tough—my father was away at war, money was tight, mother had to work, and I was left in the care of an unloving grandmother. To my little heart and mind, each of those sighs and the feelings behind them meant that I was a burden: *I* was making my mother unhappy.

Through much of my adult life, it upset me terribly whenever anyone sighed. I immediately felt guilty and experienced a tremendous urge to "make them feel better" or to run away. No amount of telling myself how silly that was brought any relief, until I realized the roots of the underlying assumption in those early hair-braiding sessions with my mother. As a child, I had lacked the awareness and sophistication to simply ask my mother if it bothered her to braid my hair; I could only take clues and fit them into my child's narrow reality. My underlying assumption became: "I'm a burden. I need to make other people happy, because it's my fault if they're not."

How do we get off the guilt train? By reminding ourselves that we aren't responsible for other people's happiness.

Let's refer once more to our old and trusted road map: Become AWARE of guilty feelings; ACKNOWLEDGE that they're there; tell someone about them; finally, ACCEPT that you feel guilty, but know that you *will* be able to choose to move away from that feeling.

Talking to others is very helpful for resolving guilt. It's amazing how quickly guilt can melt away when we receive loving feedback from people who, because *they're* less involved, can be more objective about what's happening to us.

It took me a long time to convince my guilt-prone inner child that she really didn't need to punish herself with inappropriate guilt feelings. With gentle, patient, persistent reminders, she came round to believing me. Now, she can relax and let others carry their own responsibilities. Every time something happens that would have made me feel guilty in the past, and I don't, I feel exhilarated and free.

The last time I saw the friend who'd said she had a round-trip ticket on the guilt train, she told me she no longer felt guilty. I was intrigued, and I sent her a card with a picture of a bewildered little figure carrying a suitcase. It said: "I'm going on a guilt trip. Would you mind dropping by to feed my paranoia?" Her response was:

I don't mind feeding your paranoia
anytime—since I stopped feeding (or feeding
on) my own guilt, I have more time for such
good deeds.

She had made a conscious decision to stop feeling guilty, and she succeeded. So can you.

Anger and Resentment

Scratch a woman and you find a rage.
—Virginia Woolf

Another pile of dirt that gets swept under our emotional carpets consists of anger and resentment. Anger is, for women, the ultimate taboo. We were taught not to be angry, and if we were, definitely not to express it. We learned to mask our anger, to express it in covert ways, or to hold it in dutifully until all hell breaks loose.

Stress research has established that suppressed or inappropriately expressed anger comes out in many forms, including withdrawal, ulcerated colons, migraines, child abuse, depression, and suicide.

Patricia Sun, a teacher of spirituality and conscious living, says, "Anger is our intuitive, right brain telling us, 'Whoops, something's not right here!'" Anger is a warning device. To resolve it wisely, first pay attention to it. You don't have to *do* all the things your emotionally-charged feelings suggest to you: "I'm going to hit him with a baseball bat!" Anger, if not allowed to fester and grow out of all proportion, is healthy, like a smoke alarm which, if heeded, can prevent all sorts of damage.

We ignore our anger primarily because we don't want to rock the boat. Of course, there are usually other reasons: we've been punished for being angry; we've been rejected for not "acting nice," and so on. When our conditioning prevails, anger smolders into resentment. Resentment becomes an out-of-control, irrational force which casts blame on others.

Rebecca has been married to the same man for 40 years. She has been angry many times but has only rarely expressed her feelings. When she and her husband created their patterns of married behavior, assertiveness wasn't popular. Whenever she tried to express her anger, her husband reacted with one short verbal blast and then withdrew into icy silence that lasted for days and even weeks.

Rebecca is no dummy. She learned not to say what she was feeling. But her unexpressed anger turned into smoldering resentment, which during her 40 years of marriage has expressed itself as accidents, ulcers, numerous other illnesses, and loss of interest in sex. Rebecca blames her husband for ruining her life through his uncaring attitude and her own body pays for her suppressed feelings.

Because of the general advances in awareness initiated by the women's movement, we're more aware now that it's okay to be angry, that it's natural to express our anger. We have a right to be angry, but with that right comes a responsibility to express our anger constructively.

If you express your anger in un-constructive ways, you set yourself up to feel guilty, thus creating *more* debris instead of removing some. In this case, "constructive" means "not destructive." Not expressing your anger is unhealthy. Some of us are better than others at "keeping the lid on," but sooner or later we "blow it." I like the image of a pressure cooker: the pressure builds up, and the food inside gets cooked quickly, but if you don't remember to open the little valve on top, and the steam can't escape in a controlled manner—stand back, 'cause there's going to be dinner all over the ceiling!

Once you've allowed pressure to build up to the point where it can only blow, you can't express yourself constructively. So, once again, the trick is to:

BECOME AWARE of your anger and resentment. There it is. Whether you like it or not, whether it's ladylike or not, whether it's inconvenient, uncomfortable, or whether it'll interfere with your evening, *there it is*. What is it trying to tell you?

ACKNOWLEDGE it to yourself and, if you can, to a person who can help you sort it out. It does *not* have to be expressed to the person with whom you're upset. Sometimes that's exactly the *wrong* person to talk to because, in the heat of the moment, you may say something that will cause lasting damage—or the one you're talking to may be the kind of person who could not listen to you anyway.

ACCEPT   that you have a right to your
                          anger. It's there to guide you.
                          You won't need to experience
                          resentment or guilt, if you ex-
                          press yourself constructively.

Anger can become a valuable tool if you learn to
express it well. Pull back, then ask yourself what
you want to accomplish with your anger. Do you
want to reconnect with a person? Right a wrong?
Understand a situation better? Be understood? Free
yourself from a harmful relationship?

It's *never* helpful to abuse someone physically or
emotionally. But there *are* constructive ways to release pent-up anger. When you're "steaming," it's a
good idea to release the unmanageable excess of
your anger before you confront the person you're
angry with. No one reacts receptively to a full-face
blast from the dragon's fiery jaws. An angry frontal
attack puts even the most invulnerable person on
the defensive.

I like to beat beds with a tennis racket—especially
the bed of the person I'm angry with. I know
women who go out driving on the freeway and
scream, or who throw eggs at trees. These techniques sound a little weird, but they work! (And are
lots of fun for those of us who've spent a lifetime
trying to be nice girls.) Anger creates steam: it's only
constructive to release a bit of it so that when you
open the pressure cooker nobody gets scalded.

Carol releases her anger in a way that helps her
local charities. She goes to the thrift store, buys a
bunch of old china, and goes to the trash dump and
throws plates, cups, and saucers as far and as hard

as she's able. The dump is a great choice for her crockery-smashing sessions because she doesn't feel guilty about making a mess and she doesn't have to clean up afterward. Her teenage daughter likes to go with her. Carol has been able to give herself and her daughter permission to have anger toward her ex-husband, who deserted them, and to express that anger constructively. She and her daughter usually end up laughing together—a great, healing conclusion.

It *isn't* appropriate to voice your feelings to the people concerned if you think that: you'll come away the loser; you won't be heard; you'll damage a relationship beyond repair; you'll jeopardize your job. In such cases, it's wiser to choose not to talk to the person(s).

Years ago, when I was going through my divorce and my whole life was up for review, I went through a period of feeling intense anger toward my parents. Fortunately, I chose not to share my feelings with them but rather to release those feelings in other ways, and with other people. Why was that "fortunate?" Because as I became clear about the source of my anger, I found it didn't have as much to do with my parents as I'd thought. Sure, I'd had my share of hurts in childhood—we all do. If I had blasted my parents with the full force of my anger, I might have fractured our relationship irreparably. They didn't deserve to be made the targets for all the rage and frustration I was feeling over my divorce and the events that had led up to it. However, I did choose understanding friends with whom to share my rage.

If suppressed, repressed, or destructively

expressed, anger, like a gun turned against the holder, can cripple you. If used constructively, it can be very empowering. Outrage only harms us when it becomes "inrage."

Isolation

As I begin to understand each of my clients more deeply, I hear a silent plea echoing behind their spoken words of pain: *see me, hear me, hold me.* All of us need the close contact and validation of our fellow humans. We are social beings, and when we don't experience such contact, we feel isolated and unfulfilled.

As a therapist, I see the ravages of isolation daily. People who haven't been able to share their feelings with understanding friends or families fall into chronic feelings of isolation that gather like huge piles of unresolved emotional debris, turning eventually into life-threatening despair.

A certain amount of solitude is essential. Isolation is something completely different. We need to feel part of other people and the groups with whom we live and work, to feel attached to, identified with them—not in a dependent relationship but in a grounded, rooted, mutually helpful way. Churches, families, schools, self-help groups, and friends all help break up feelings of isolation.

Many of us began to feel isolated early in life. If our parents misunderstood, criticized, teased, or judged us, we began to fear sharing ourselves with others. The world felt unsafe. If our parents didn't see, hear, or hold us, or if they loved us only when we were doing things "right," we began to feel that even if it *were* safe to share our real feelings, we weren't worthy to do so. We grew up and became adults who didn't want to "burden others with our troubles," or "air our dirty laundry in public."

We pay dearly for our silence. Isolation is a form of emotional suicide.

People in the bereavement groups I lead are astounded by how much better they feel, once they share their pain with others and learn that they are not alone or unique in their reactions. Their isolation is broken; connections form; healing begins.

Frequently, in our isolation, we feel unaccepted and unacceptable. We feel we're different, the only ones who feel a certain way. Everyone else looks squared-away and happy; we're the weird ones. We develop a socially suitable facade behind which we hide our true feelings. We become social chameleons, changing faces to suit different situations and people. To a certain extent, all of us do this because we all feel frightened to reveal how vulnerable we are in certain situations!

Dr. Pauline Rose Clance, in her book, *The Imposter Phenomenon: Overcoming the Fear that Haunts Your Success*, shows that none of us have a flawless self-concept. She writes: "I constantly see men and women (especially women) who have every right to be on top of the world, but instead they're miserable because in their eyes they never measure up. They feel fraudulent."

No matter how successful we are, or how loved, many of us hear a whispering, convincing voice inside that reminds us of our faults and failings. The way to transform that inner saboteur is to learn to love and accept ourselves *as we are*. We need to come to an understanding of the part of us that is judgmental and tries so terribly hard to be perfect. Madame Marie Curie said, "Nothing in life is to be feared. It is only to be understood." In our confusion, we fear that our faults and weaknesses are unforgivable, so we isolate ourselves behind a mask.

Breaking out of isolation takes courage. If your isolation is a long-standing habit, give yourself time to go forward slowly and safely.

I referred earlier to Victoria, a victim of violent sexual child abuse. She protected herself and others from her terrifying secret for many years. Even now, she only feels safe talking about her traumatic experiences if her legs are drawn up tightly under her chin. Her physical withdrawal reflects her emotional withdrawal. If she gives herself that safety now, a day will come when she'll feel comfortable talking in a more relaxed position.

If we aren't gentle and kind to ourselves as we risk change, we merely reinforce the conviction that the world *isn't* a safe place.

Explore the reasons why you isolate yourself. What are you protecting? What do you fear? Find people with whom you can take off your mask—people who're willing to see, hear, and hold you. By all means, avoid "throwing your (emotional) pearls before swine." Swine are people who say things like, "You *shouldn't* feel that way." Or, "That's stupid—why don't you just (_____)?" Swine make you wish you'd kept your mouth shut. Be discerning about those with whom you take off your protective mask. You very much need—and deserve—empathetic, kind understanding.

Remind yourself that you carry around an inner child who feels that being isolated is the only safe way to live. Why is she frightened? Can she count on you to protect her? Be a loving parent to your inner child.

Become loving and honest with yourself, too. None of us is perfect! We all have our share of inner squiggly worms (and some boa constrictors). The more we can honestly and gently be vulnerable with others, the more we can free ourselves from our fears and foibles.

None of us is completely free of inner debris. We've all grieved. We all carry around unresolved emotional junk. We've all suppressed anger, guilt, and resentment. We're human, and these experiences help us to grow. But we can only grow and be who we really are by finishing our "business," by healing our inner hurts, sharing our pain, and forgiving ourselves and others. If we leave piles of unresolved emotional debris under the rug, there's always the danger that we may stumble over them.

In order to give up being a Designated Garbage Can and a Responsibility Sponge for everyone, you'll need to begin to move beyond inner isolation.

Growth involves risk; but if you increase your ability to tolerate pain, you'll be able to risk acting even when you're afraid—my definition of courage. As you clean the debris out from under your carpet, you'll feel an increasing sense of freedom and creativity. Not immediately, perhaps, because it takes time for the healing process to gain force and momentum. But if you work at it consistently and with patience, your healing will begin, and your creativity and freedom will start to flow.

Writing this book has been risky and scary for me. For months I wouldn't let anybody read it. When I mailed the first chapters to my business manager, my stomach felt as if it had been shoved in the mail box too. But the book became a healing outlet for fears and limitations that I've experienced for years.

Do yourself a healing favor: find a creative outlet for your pain. One of the best ways to sweep away old fear-debris and break isolation is to reach out in honesty, love, and service to someone else—not because we "should" or as a bitter sacrifice, but as an invitation to a loving bond and a mutual boost to ourselves and the other person(s). To live happy, fulfilled lives, we all need to serve from our "overflow." I'll talk more about that in Chapter 13.

*It is not the end of the physical body
that should worry us. Rather,
our concern must be to live while we're alive—
to release our inner selves
from the spiritual death
that comes with living behind a facade
designed to conform to external definitions
of who and what we are.*

—ELISABETH KUBLER-ROSS

CHAPTER 8

The Leveled Life

MANY OF US CARRY around unresolved grief in the form of a feeling that we're somehow "missing out" on life, that life is passing us by. Life, which had promised to be so exciting, full of joy and surprises, has turned out to feel about as level and barren as the salt flats.

One of the biggest words in a flat, "leveled" life is "If":

> *If only I'd . . .*
> *If only I hadn't . . .*
> *If only they . . .*
> *If only I'd known . . .*
> *If only, if only, if only . . .*

"If" comes from Ignorance teamed up with Fear: *Ignorance* of possibilities in life and *Fear* of taking the risks involved in seizing those opportunities.

Children are natural, born risk-takers. They move out into the world and toward others with their arms wide open. For children, life is full of mountains and valleys waiting to be explored. There's nothing "level" about the life of a healthy, spontaneous child: one moment she'll be rolling around in a fit of glee; the next moment, she's grabbing aggressively for her toy and sobbing.

When we see a child acting "level" and flat, we take her temperature. Why, then, do we feel it's okay for *us* to ooze through life on a boring, uniform level? What, after all, is "okay" about a life that's safe but lacks wonder, enthusiasm, anger, and joy? What's "normal" about living from a place within ourselves that knows no spontaneous gratitude, sense of rightness, and harmony with the "scheme of things"?

We fall into the habit of living "blah" lives so gradually that we aren't aware of how flat and tasteless our lives have become. When my first husband left me, I realized how level my life was. When the shock wore off, I experienced an explosion of feelings. I'd be low, then I'd skyrocket in a frenzy of rage and desire for revenge. I'd be thinking of suicide, then I'd be giddy with fantasies about the possibilities that lay open before me.

During the years it took to heal those wounds, I experienced a wider range of feelings than I'd had since I was a teenager. Thus, I became AWARE of how flat my life had become. I ACKNOWLEDGED it, ACCEPTED the reality of the pain it had brought, and CHOSE to do something about it. One of my first, fleeting choices was: "I'm never going to let myself be hurt like this again. Never, never, never!" To protect myself, I locked myself up in an emotional bubble-dome, out of reach and invulnerable. But that didn't last long because I soon began to understand my own role in the breakup: in my discontent, I had leveled my own life.

During that first marriage, I hadn't been willing to be aware of what was going on. It was simply too scary. I became funny on the outside, covertly and ineffectually venting my anger by telling witty but barbed stories. Later, when I was able to see my actions without flinching, but with love and forgiveness, I chose to act differently. I took back my promise "never to be hurt again" and replaced it with two affirmations that I still live by.

The first was: "I choose to *live*." For me, that meant a commitment to risk-taking and to experiencing *all* of my feelings, whether joyous, painful or indifferent. I had tried to avoid pain all my life; now I was learning that in order to live I had to embrace life's whole package: pain, joy—the entire gamut of my feelings. It wasn't a decision I made lightly or easily.

I was helped immensely by this passage from Gibran's *The Prophet*:

> Your joy is your sorrow unmasked
> And the selfsame well from which your laughter
>   rises was oftentimes filled with your tears
> And how else can it be?
> The deeper that sorrow carves into your being,
> the more joy you can contain.

My second choice was: "I will never give myself away again." Giving yourself away depletes you until you no longer feel there *is* a you. Please note: *giving* is not the same as *giving yourself away*. Freely giving fulfills you and creates *more* of you.

The Higher You Go, the Farther You'll Fall

Many of us hold the image that life is a pie. It's dished out in large and small pieces, and when it's gone, it's gone. Therefore, we don't "tempt the gods" by asking for too much; after all, if we ask for more than our share, we're just begging to be disappointed.

When we were children, and the joy of risking and stretching was still natural to us, we were warned:

- *Don't get too excited.*
- *Remember, there are only two spots on the cheerleading squad and 14 girls trying out for them.*
- *Don't get your heart set on it.*
- *You'll cry as hard tomorrow as you laugh today.*
- *Don't expect too much from (＿＿＿＿＿＿)*
  (marriage is a good fill-in for that one!).
- *Life is hard.*
- *Don't rock the boat.*

What are the underlying messages behind such statements? Try these:

- *It's dangerous to risk.*
- *It's dangerous to hope, to be happy, to expect*

life to be good and fulfilling.
- *There isn't ever enough to go around.*
- *Give up your childlike awe and wonder.*

We are trained to believe that *the higher you go, the farther you'll fall.*

I know a woman whose favorite statement is: "Life is hard and then you die." What's your image of a woman whose life is determined by such a statement? Is her life constantly threatened by scarcity? Yes. Does she cling to the old because risk-taking is scary? Yes. This woman believes that life is hard, and so for her it jolly well is. She gets what she believes life will give her.

If you're one of the older children in your family, can you remember the birth of your first younger sibling? I do. I remember being both excited and scared. Would my parents have enough love for both of us? They assured me they would, so I began to look forward to *my* baby. Then my grandmother gave me this input, which was all too easy for a seven-year-old to take to heart: "Even though your mother and daddy will now have someone they love more than you, *I'll* still love you." You can imagine how I welcomed my baby sister after that: with open hostility. Because I believed I'd be un-loved, I *felt* unloved. I *was* loved, but for many crucial years I was unable to feel it; and this scarcity of feeling loved contributed much toward the leveling of my life in adulthood. It was only with the loving help of friends, my mother, and therapy that I was eventually healed.

Linda's family gave her the message that she must "do it right or don't do it at all!" She was never given permission to learn, risk, and experiment, so she developed a pattern she called "slip 'n' quit." Since nobody does things right the first time, and since she had never been encouraged to make mistakes, had no support system to buoy her up while her life jacket was in repair, she took up a whole series of things in which she "slipped and quit," including ice skating and ballet.

Linda was afraid to climb higher for fear of falling farther. Her habit of "slipping and quitting" fostered a fear of trying, so she settled for less and less, shedding dreams almost before she was fully conscious of them. Her life became level.

Linda's story has a happy ending: as she became AWARE of her pattern, ACKNOWLEDGED it to herself and to me, and ACCEPTED herself as she was, she was able to CHOOSE to change, to "do it even if she did it wrong." Linda became a loving parent to herself and gradually acquired much more courage to be who she really is. I saw her recently, and she was glowing with enthusiasm about a new job and the overflow of energy she felt for the job as well as for other areas of her life. She told me she still slipped, but that she had been able to promise herself not to quit.

Safe But Sorry

When we settle for less in order to feel safe, we always feel sorry. If we compromise our dreams, limiting ourselves with negative ideas gleaned in childhood or adulthood, if we accept that it's useless to ask for what we want and need, if we believe lack is safer than abundance, our lives will close around us like a safe but suffocating blanket.

There are few greater griefs than being forced to admit that our lives have been a series of compromises that have left us feeling dull and out of touch with our dreams. My father used to tell me when I was feeling low: "It's just a little valley on the highway of life." I didn't much appreciate that then, but I've since come to understand how right he was. If we are to enjoy the "high ways" of life, we need to learn from and grow in the valleys.

We do need security, but security can be purchased at too high a price. Security obtained at the expense of exhilarating, creative growth and change merely strangles us. Surely the caterpillar feels secure in its cocoon—but when it emerges, it needs to unfold its wings and risk flight.

Give up any addiction to being safe but sorry. Resolve your grief over the leveling of your life by using the three A's. Take flight. Have the courage to **SOAR:** *Stretch Out And Risk.*

It isn't for the moment you are struck
that you need courage,
but for the long uphill climb
back to sanity and faith and security.

—ANNE MORROW LINDBERGH

CHAPTER 9

Natural Grief

N O MATTER HOW RICH our life, how bright our future, we all experience grief. To live is to change and be vulnerable to loss. Loss brings grief.

Grief takes two forms: natural grief and unresolved grief. Natural grieving is allowing yourself to experience your feelings and move through them *at the time* of loss. This process is cleansing and leads to full recovery.

Unresolved grief is created when you don't allow yourself to work through feelings as they arise. You shelve them, but they don't simply evaporate; they gnaw at your energy, prey on your emotions, and generally debilitate you.

Loss:
Both Inevitable and Ordinary

Sooner or later, we'll all experience loss. A loved one will die. A child will leave home. A dream will remain unfulfilled. Our hair will turn grey, our faces will wrinkle, and our underarms will wiggle. Change is unavoidable and often creates grief.

How well we heal will be determined largely by how clearly we recognize our grief and let ourself experience it, so that the natural process of unraveling the pain can take place.

There are some subtle losses that we wrongly tend to slough off as unimportant. My partner and I had been looking for office space for more than a year when we found what appeared to be the ideal place: a beautiful new building in the pines. The owners promised that we could design our own space. That prospect was great since there were two things we especially required: excellent sound proofing and equal square footage for each office. It looked easy. Being a lover of design, I stayed up most of a night working out an arrangement that we both liked. We took it to the architect, who altered it to suit his aesthetic eye. During the construction, I kept saying that my office was smaller than the other. There was lots of talk about outside versus inside measurements, usable space, spaces expanding and contracting during building stages, etc. They were the same, I was assured.

Not so. The finished offices have inadequate sound-proofing and unequal square footage. One of the major aspects of my grieving about this, which I discovered as I sorted out my feelings of rage and disappointment, was one that we women have endured for centuries: the men involved had simply not *listened*. They had placated, promised, patted us on the head, and then done what *they* felt was best. Our concerns had not been taken seriously. We had been *devalued*!

In the confrontation that followed, the architect admitted that he *had* moved a couple of walls and that, yes, the space was unequal but that the bigger office needed the extra space because of its shape. He may have been right in principle, but the point was that *we* were not asked for our input. The decision was made without us and in contradiction of our specific requirements.

The office situation made me aware how tired I was of grieving over issues of powerlessness. My grief was symbolic of the devaluation women have experienced for centuries. I am, finally, willing to quit passively lamenting my "fate" and instead to be assertive (not aggressive) about what I want and need and how I expect to be treated. We now have adequate soundproofing and have definitely been *heard* concerning our anger and frustration about the square footage. I have made peace with my smaller office.

The experience taught me a great deal about how standing up for ourselves, finishing our business, and grieving over loss leads to healing and cleans up debris that blocks the flow of life's energy.

Unfinished Business

The members of my bereavement groups have taught me that nothing blocks healing more than unfinished business. Many people say:

"If only I had said (_____) or
done (_____)! Now I can never
say or do (_____)!"

Unfinished business is anything you regret not having done, said, or felt—or something you regret *having* said, done, or felt. Jesus was referring to finishing our business when he said:

If it should happen therefore that while you are presenting your offering upon the altar, and right there you remember that your brother has any grievance against you, leave your offering there upon the altar, and first go and make peace with your brother, and then come back and present your offering.

There are lots of reasons why we leave our business unfinished. We were told as we grew up: "Don't make mountains out of mole hills," "Stop being so emotional," and "Don't rock the boat." We learned to keep quiet, to hold back our feelings rather than express them. We learned, in effect, to create unfinished business.

In our fast-paced lives we often live in the past or future, not paying much attention to *now*. Our unfinished business originates in the NOW. Sins of omission are created when we are not present in the current moment. You can't escape grief and loss, but by taking care of business as it presents itself in your life, you can make sure that when loss comes you won't be burdened by regrets and "if-only's."

To deal with the unfinished business you've already gathered:

1. Understand and resolve it; or,
2. Let it go.

Make a list of your unfinished business. Who needs to be told that you love them? With whom do you need to talk over a misunderstanding? Which practical jobs need to be finished? Which unattained goals still need to be achieved? What hurts do you need to heal?

Divide your list into three sections and label them:

1. BUSINESS I CONTROL

This is "old business" that you can choose either to finish or to let go. The decision to let old business go should be made in a spirit of conscious, clear choice, not by chickening out or rationalizing. You let it go because it is truly no longer an issue in your life. If you can't get a free and clear feeling about letting an item of unfinished business go, it probably means you need to finish it. If you choose to finish some business, make a list of ways to achieve that. If it seems impossible, seek help.

For years, Jim had carried a guilty fear that he'd been responsible for the deaths of his father and grandmother. Just before each of their deaths, he'd been angry at them and had wished that they would die. Having come to me with what he believed was an unrelated problem, he quickly became aware of that unresolved guilt. Eventually, he was able to understand why he'd felt as he had at the time of the deaths and to forgive himself and let the guilt go.

2. BUSINESS INVOLVING ANOTHER PERSON

This is tricky because even if you do *your* part, the other person may neither understand nor cooperate. Louise knew that there was unfinished business in her relationship with her father. She spent time with him, hugged him, and tried to talk to him. He patiently endured her attentions, turned to stone when she hugged him, and read the paper or watched TV while she tried to talk. She began to understand that he was terrified of intimacy and that it was his fear, not her unworthiness, that kept them at a distance. Because she felt good reaching out to him, she continued to do so, though she laid aside her expectation of mutual give and take. *Her* business, at least, was finished.

Over time, Louise's father began to feel safe in responding to her efforts, and they are becoming closer. Remember, though, that some people will simply be incapable of responding to your efforts to finish old business. Still, if you do your part, you, at least, will feel free.

In deciding on a course of action, don't base your success on whether the other person responds in a certain manner. Find out what your role is in clearing up the old business. If you "go and make peace" with your friend, and peace isn't something your friend is open to, that will be *their* unfinished business, not yours. A helpful technique for releasing old business is to write out all the ways you wish a situation or a relationship had turned out and all of your negative feelings about it, then burn the paper.

Ask that your feelings be changed and healed with the symbolic destruction of them on the paper.

3. BUSINESS OVER WHICH I HAVE NO CONTROL

Take your choice: when confronted with old business over which you have no control, you can fret and stew, thus creating mountains of new debris in your life, or you can seek the help of a friend or therapist in finishing it by *accepting* the way things are.

When I need to accept and let go of something I can't control, I find this old, familiar prayer very helpful:

SERENITY PRAYER
God, grant me the Serenity
to accept the things
I cannot change
The Courage to change
the things I can
And the Wisdom
to know the difference.

Recognizing and Unraveling the Pain

When you're in the middle of the grieving process, it feels as if you're the only person in the world who has ever experienced such intense pain. But grief is, in fact, so common that Dr. Elisabeth Kubler-Ross, a foremost authority on death and bereavement, has formulated five stages which are normal during the grieving process. Knowing the stages we may go through helps us make sense of our pain. The stages are:

1. Shock and denial	*"It can't be true!"*
2. Anger	*"Why me?"*
3. Bargaining	*"I'll do anything!"*
4. Depression	*"What's the use?"*
5. Acceptance	*"I don't like it, but I can handle it."*

After a loss, we will experience some or all of these stages. Looking back to the time when I confronted the possibility of divorce from my first husband, I can see that I experienced them all.

1. Shock and denial	*"No, I'm sure he won't leave . . . family is too important to him."*
2. Anger	*"How dare you do this to us! I'll make you pay!"*
3. Bargaining	*"How have I failed you? What do you want from me? I'll do anything."*
4. Depression	*"I can't go on. I have no life outside of this one. I'm a failure as a woman. There's never been a divorce in our family. How can I make it financially and emotionally?"*
5. Acceptance	*"I am making it. I'll go back to school. I can be happy without him. I can take care of myself."*

Remember that when you face a loss, whether large or small, your tendency will be to try to avoid the pain inherent in each of the stages. No wonder! The pain of grief winds itself around your vital organs and squeezes the very breath out of you. I don't mean that you allow yourself to wallow in self-pity. Far from it—I mean that you allow yourself to feel the pain, thereby letting it unravel its grip on your heart. Healing can come only from letting your pain roll over and around you just as breathing and flowing with labor pains helps you to cooperate with your body in the birth of a child.

Talk about your pain. Share it. Cry over it. Read about loss and grieving. Be especially careful of your body, which will be weaker and more vulnerable while you grieve. *Don't* try to cover up your grief with a plastered-on "all's well" face. Pace yourself to recovery; don't try to do business as usual. Realize that you've been hit by an emotion truck or, if your loss is smaller, by a VW. You may need to grieve for five minutes, five weeks, or in diminishing intensity, for five years, and that "time is the healer." It may hardly seem possible while you grieve, but if you allow yourself to grieve, you *will* heal.

Part Four

Limits And Boundaries: "I Have Rights!! Okay?"

*When you make a world
tolerable for yourself
you make a world
tolerable for others.*

—ANAIS NIN

Limits And Boundaries: "I Have Rights!! Okay?"

WOMEN ARE WAKING UP to the realization that they *do* have rights. They're beginning, tentatively and sometimes militantly, to act on that realization. I have a cartoon that depicts the difficulty of the process: a woman is sitting at a restaurant table with a man. She says: "I have independence! I ask for what I need. I am taking responsibility for my life." In the final drawing, she reaches across the table and grabs the man by the arms: "Is that okay with you?"

Throughout history, women have been considered men's helpmates, secretaries, and moral supporters. *Behind* every successful man, as the saying goes, stands a good woman. Fortunately, we're living in an age in which that outdated saying is being changed to: "Side by side stand successful men and women."

Although we may accept and *believe in* our equality with deep mental conviction, we may need to work hard on our ability to honor our limits and boundaries—to stand up for our rights and *really feel* that we can expect such treatment as kindness, respect, and thoughtfulness. As we learn to honor our equality and begin to be AWARE of our limits and boundaries, we can ACKNOWLEDGE them to ourselves and others, ACCEPT that we have a right to them, and *choose* to express ourselves in creative, new ways.

We are changing the way we express our desire for equality. Instead of speaking either belligerently or defensively we are responding to a firm inner conviction that we simply *are* equal. With that belief we can now express ourselves as equals.

What Are Limits and Boundaries?

Let's approach the question through the back door. Have you ever found yourself accepting the unacceptable—i.e., acquiescing to unkind, disrespectful treatment that makes you feel devalued?

Whenever you receive that kind of treatment in silent suffering or whine and beg ineffectually to be treated better, you ignore your limits and permit others to invade the boundaries of your self-respect.

When people need something, do they always call on "good old you" and know you will come through even if you've just come home from 10 days in intensive care? When you let others take advantage of you, you aren't honoring your limits.

Whenever you say "yes" when you're dying to say "no," you aren't communicating your limits honestly, and you're setting yourself up to feel resentful, hostile, and depressed. You'll adopt either of two modus operandi, withdrawing from others or blowing your top. Not being honest about your personal limits and boundaries creates feelings of betrayal, anger, defensiveness, and bewilderment.

Learning to stand up for yourself and honor your limits and boundaries involves first, noticing when you're being taken advantage of; and second, giving yourself PERMISSION to *have* and to *honor* your limits and boundaries. In order to have fair and open relationships with others, you must learn how to communicate your limits and boundaries honestly.

*A woman's public identity
is her husband's
and her private identity,
her children's.*

—VIRGINIA WOOLF

CHAPTER 10

Giving Ourselves Away

AMONG the people you know, including yourself, who gets their wants and needs met most read-
ily? Make an impromptu list of your acquaintances,
either on paper or in your mind. Include among the
wants and needs both tangible desires and intangi-
bles such as receiving respect, being heard, and
having opinions valued. Is there anyone on the list
who *always* gets what s/he asks for? Are there some
persons who are more than likely to get what they
want? Where are *you* on the list? If you're near the
bottom, you're probably giving yourself away.

Maria lived for 19 years with an emotionally abusive husband. She endured being put down privately and publicly and learned to "laugh it off."
Having been raised a Catholic and holding staunch

no-divorce views, she felt she had no choice but to accept her fate; thus, she gave herself away and came to loathe both herself and her husband.

We may give ourselves away in big chunks (not returning to school because that would inconvenience somebody) or small chunks (not speaking up when we're hurt or annoyed). Take a look at the following list of questions. If you can answer "yes" to any of them, you're probably giving yourself away:

1. Do you have self-limiting fears?
2. Are you often filling the wants and needs of others without having your own needs met?
3. Do you say "yes" when you'd like to say "no"?
4. Are decisions difficult for you?
5. Are your close relationships unsatisfying?
6. Do you lack self-confidence?
7. Are you your own worst critic?
8. Are you overly tired most of the time?
9. Does your life have little joy and spontaneous laughter?

Women who give themselves away have a hard time making decisions because they're afraid that someone else might consider them stupid if they make a mistake. When I separated from my first husband, I needed to buy a car. I looked at several, but felt unable to choose one. I asked my husband for his advice—an okay thing to do if you ask as an equal. But I considered his opinion more valuable and wise than my own. My intuition was screaming, "No, no, no!" but I ignored it and bought the car he'd chosen.

That car and I were enemies from the very start. By not heeding my inner voice, I had given myself away. If I had had the courage to heed my inner voice and had made the decision for myself, I would have come away feeling better about my integrity-and maybe I'd have had a better car!

Habitually feeling NO but saying YES is a good indication we are giving ourselves away.

Saying "Yes" But Feeling "No"

Ever come away from the phone after having said "yes" to 48 dozen cookies for a Halloween party, the chairpersonship of two committees, and extra work hours that conflicted with plans of your own?

Afterwards, you feel you could cut out your tongue, die, or at least develop some highly contagious disease. Feeling like that means you've just given yourself away.

What in the world impels us to say "yes" when we feel "no"? In a word: we think we "should." We're afraid of what *they* will think of us if we say "no." Yet I've discovered that when I really feel I have a right to say "no" and say it with full awareness of that right, people think it's just fine. When we expect people to accept our "no's" and to honor our limits and boundaries, they generally do. Our conviction that we have the right to choose to say "no" comes across and is accepted. Replace the draining "should" with empowering words like *can*, *want to*, *choose to*, or *will*.

A key method for having your "no's" heard is to choose one statement and stick with it:

You: I can't chair this particular committee. I'm sorry.

They:	Oh, please! I don't have *anyone* else I can call.
You:	I know that's hard, but I cannot do it at this time of year.
They:	I don't know what I'll do. I'm desperate.
You:	It really is hard to organize this stuff, isn't it? I'm really sorry I can't help you right now.

Notice that the "you" person in the scenario stuck to the statement, "I can't," thereby honoring her limits and boundaries while expressing compassion for the other person's problem. "You" did not give herself away.

Before you say "yes," take several deep breaths. Ask yourself if you're merely saying "yes" out of guilt and fear. Tell yourself that you have the *right* to choose. Pause! If you need time to consider your alternatives, call the person back. You don't have to let yourself be terrorized by other people's expectations of you.

The Terror of Expectations

Your own expectations and the expectations of others can kill you emotionally. All of us—women, men, children, young and old—have suffered under the tyranny of expectations. Didn't we expect our honeymoons to be romantic and idyllic? Few are.

I recently saw a scene from a play in which one of the characters gave this wonderful commentary on expectations: she was talking to a classmate at a high school reunion, and she said, "I thought that once he and I got together, things would change. By the way, that's what's written over the Women's Entrance to Hell: *'Things Will Change!'"*

So much of what we expect is sheer fantasy. We expect to be able to make our families happy. (Our families expect us to make them happy, too.) We expect ourselves to be always bright, cheerful, and healthy. We expect ourselves to be always attractive, always nurturing, always ready with wisdom and comfort. Expectations are exhausting, not to speak of terrifying and paralyzing.

How can we possibly live up to our own and others' expectations? Jordan and Margaret Paul, in their book *Do I Have to Give Up Me to be Loved by You?*, talk about their evolution as a couple:

> *Margaret has become aware of the beliefs that led her to assume responsibility for the emotional well-being of our family members, thus limiting the spiritual growth of Jordan and our children, as well as herself. Jordan has looked at his beliefs that made Margaret responsible for his happiness and he has seen how this led to his judging her behavior as unloving whenever she did something that upset him. His avoidance of personal responsibility and the anger he felt when his expectations weren't met led to many relationship problems as well as much of his own unhappiness.*

One of the most crippling things we can do to ourselves is to expect someone else to make us happy. Other people can only help to bring out what is already within us: the capacity to feel good about ourselves, to feel useful, to feel loved. When we feel unhappy and unfulfilled "because" of others, we can be sure we're giving ourselves away. We then need to take a long look at the beliefs and expectations we hold which are keeping us dependent on others.

Maria (the woman who was raised a Catholic and who was emotionally abused by her husband) woke up one morning and said, "Enough!" To save her life emotionally, she left her husband. Unfortunately, having taken so long to realize that she had other choices, she was forced to leave her two children behind. Had she honored her limits and boundaries sooner, her marriage might have been salvaged—but so many years of swallowed anger had created scars that were too deep, and it was too late.

Notice that there's a delicate difference between *asking for* what we want and need and *expecting* others to follow a hidden script we've written for them. By adhering too rigidly to our own, interiorized picture of how things "should be," we activate normal, healthy rebellion in the other person.

My husband and I had a fairy-tale romance: we met in Hawaii and courted across the Pacific. It was perfect . . . *we* were perfect, confident that we'd been sprinkled with fairy dust and that our relationship would be forever blissful. Of course, it wasn't. After we'd settled into an everyday routine, our expectations of unending bliss began to get in the way of our real lives.

As a novice marriage counselor with a divorce in my background, I felt I had a pretty realistic picture of what my new marriage *had* to be, to be acceptable. My husband's wants, needs, and images differed significantly from mine. It took a long time and a lot of grieving to realize that I was smothering our relationship with my expectations. I was activating my husband's rebel personality with my "it has to be this way" script. After a great deal of inner struggle, I was able to stop terrorizing both of us with my idealistic expectations.

Then, a funny thing happened: after a cooling-off period, when he trusted that I had really gotten off his back, he began to be the way I'd demanded that he be earlier. Since I'd released those expectations and found other ways to fulfill those needs, his change was much appreciated (the chocolate chips in the cookie of life) but no longer necessary for my emotional survival.

In even the most stable and caring relationship, there will be unmet expectations. I may expect a quiet evening of firelight and intimate sharing, and he'll expect to watch basketball. We both may expect our kids for dinner, and they'll want to go have pizza with friends. We simply can't survive emotionally if we expect to have every expectation fulfilled. Life just isn't set up that way; so the healthiest response is to stay very flexible and not take it personally when our expectations aren't met.

The Superwoman Syndrome

Whatever women do they must do twice as well as men to be thought half as good. Luckily, this is not difficult.
—Charlotte Whitton

Being flexible and being a doormat aren't the same thing. One of the ways we give ourselves away is in trying to be everything to everybody: playing the omnipresent, omnicompetent Superwoman.

Superwoman's cape is lined with guilt and trimmed with fear . . . fear that she won't live up to others' expectations and guilt when she doesn't. The self-defined Superwoman can never fly: her expectations are rarely met, and even when they are, she merely replaces them with higher and ever-unattainable new ones.

I had a client who'd raised three children alone. Now she's remarried, and she's raising a stepchild and three emotionally disturbed adopted siblings. She makes nearly all their clothes, cooks all the family's meals from scratch, balances a budget that would send chills up a contortionist's spine, and remains extremely active in her church. She used to get very upset when she occasionally felt unloving.

This woman's own background was one of trauma and deprivation, a history which had left her with deep emotional scars and a tremendous case of Superwoman Syndrome. She never felt that she compared favorably to other people. She berated herself for a bewildering variety of real and imagined small failures. I used to get exhausted listening to her tell about just *one* of her three adopted children and his deviant behavior.

Little by little, she was able to create a small sign to hang over her soul, at least some of the time:

SUPERWOMAN
DOESN'T
LIVE HERE
ANYMORE

Women who are caught in the stranglehold of the Superwoman Syndrome are often driven by economic necessity, as well as by personal desire, to hold down a full-time job *outside* the home and a full-time job *inside* also. Whether we are career women, at-home women, or both, we are often prodded mercilessly by an inner dragon to be perfect. Many of us look outside ourselves for self-esteem. (A contradiction in terms, when you think about it.) Turning to others to mirror our value back to us, to keep us filled up with worth, inevitably leaves us feeling used and invaded.

Once a man is on hand,
a woman tends to stop
believing in her own beliefs.

—COLETTE DOWLING

CHAPTER 11

Allowing Ourselves To Be Invaded

Y OU ARE ALLOWING yourself to be invaded: if you fill the wants and needs of others and resent that your own needs are not met; if you doubt your ability to make decisions and therefore acquiesce whenever someone says, "No, no, I think you should do (_____)"; if your children, mate, co-workers, and friends feel free to borrow your things without asking your permission.

We become vulnerable to invasion through fear: fear of rejection, imperfection, embarrassment, confrontation. Because we fear other people's reactions, we allow them to violate our limits and boundaries. We *all* have limits and boundaries, and our physical and emotional responses tell us when someone has trespassed on our private selves.

Being invaded brings feelings of being taken advantage of, of having to *give up* something. If one of my children goes into my bathroom and borrows my hair brush without asking, I feel invaded, as if I'd given up the right to have my things where and when I want them. The child has stepped past a boundary that has been clearly spelled out, and I get angry and feel resentful.

When you've just settled into a warm bath after a hard day at work, and the kids bang on the door for you to settle a disagreement, whether you'll be invaded or not will depend upon your reaction. If, because of a false sense of responsibility for their happiness, you leap out of the tub and rush to solve their problems, you've been invaded. I know women who say they *never* have a moment of time to themselves because of the demands of their jobs and families. One woman told me she constantly feels as if she's being "nibbled to death by ducks."

It's not outer circumstances that keep these women going at a killing pace but the demands they place on themselves through their addiction to the Superwoman Syndrome. While it's true that the demands on a woman to play many roles are stressful, we *do* have the right to make choices. Only by healing the fears that keep us from believing we have rights can we begin to honor our limits and boundaries and thus truly act for the highest good of ourselves and others. Then we will no longer allow ourselves to be invaded.

Footprints on Our Faces

When I was in high school, I gave my best friend the nickname "Footprint" because she allowed her boyfriend to walk all over her. I'm sure I deserved the name, too, for the way I behaved with some of the boys I dated. My friend and I felt vaguely uncomfortable and powerless behaving like doormats, but this was the 1950's, when girls were encouraged to cater to boys.

I remember reading a series of little YWCA books on dating, menstruating, and the art of making a proper phone call. The booklet on dating actually said that in order to be popular (that summit of adolescent values!), a girl should encourage the boys talk about themselves. The booklet said to ask boys leading questions that would get them started talking on topics of interest to *them*. To build the boy's interest in *me*, I was to feign an interest in cars and sports or whatever that particular boy liked.

Surely those books had been reprinted from volumes discovered in some moldy, pre-Victorian attic! I remember thinking, "Isn't that a stupid game? What if there's a subject *I'd* like to talk about?" My doubts manifested themselves in an interesting way: I developed a chronic frog in my throat; especially when out on a date, I felt that I would choke at any minute. Often I'd need to excuse myself to find a private place to hack and cough. I was literally choking on the words I was holding back and the game-like words I spoke. More basically, I was choking on the underlying message from those how-to-get-along-with-boys suggestions: "You aren't as important as *they* are." I carried that semi-hidden belief that I was second rate with me into adulthood. I also carried my throat frog.

A few years ago I filled in an assertiveness inventory in a magazine. Since I had already taken my Master's in psychology, had been through a very growth-producing divorce, and felt I'd made great progress in developing self-esteem, I was shocked and angered when I tested fairly assertive in all areas except in my relations with the men I loved, including my two sons.

In fact, I had to admit that I *was* acting out a lingering assumption that men are better, deserve to be listened to more than women, and would probably leave me if I didn't take a back seat to them in most matters. I allowed men to invade me by firmly planting their tennies on my face. "Croak!" Significantly, my need to clear my throat was a family joke and, I learned later, a constant irritation to my husband.

I decided to do something about it. I began to assert myself with men, even with the men I loved. I ferreted out my hidden attitudes of subservience and stopped giving myself away. The process was not easy and required the help of a good therapist, supportive friends, clients, and my own stick-to-itiveness.

The frog in my throat, which had been with me constantly for 28 years, disappeared. Now, if I begin to choke and croak, I look for ways in which I've slipped and allowed myself to be invaded. Froggie has become a friend.

Roles to Conquer the Invader

One of the primary urges people need to fulfill in their lives is the desire to have and to express their own personal power. Thus, when we feel invaded or taken advantage of, we immediately seek ways to "win" over the threatening invader. Since society hasn't encouraged women to develop their power (it isn't feminine, you know), we adopted secret and dishonest means of having and using power. The trouble with deviousness, though, is that in the long run, everyone who adopts it loses.

These are some of the secret roles women have adopted:

MOTHER

There are just three times in our lives when we need to be mothered: in infancy, senility, and when ill. The rest of the time, we need to develop our own inner capacity to be strong and take care of ourselves. Yet women have chosen to mother men, despite the thoroughly proven fact that an overly motherly attitude is death to romantic love or the love between equal marriage partners.

I often find myself having to tell my women clients to "monitor their Mom-isms." A Mom-ism expresses itself in ways as trivial as telling a driver where to park. "Why don't you park by the bank?" You may say that this is just being helpful, but in the driver's mind it most likely will be taken as patronizing, as being unnecessarily taken care of, as being considered a stupid, incapable child. No one really enjoys being told that s/he can't perform simple actions like deciding where to park the car. If help is asked for, that's different. Another Mom-ism is nagging: "Have you done (_____) yet?"

To be fair, there's another side to the Mom-ism coin: the man's tendency to play Little Boy in an effort to get a woman to play the role of a mother who'll take care of him and fulfill him inwardly. The Mom/Little Boy syndrome is one of the most significant factors in failing marriages today. Among the couples I see professionally, it's epidemic. And the only way to stop it is to become AWARE of it, ACKNOWLEDGE it, ACCEPT it, and then CHOOSE to STOP IT! Even if it takes leaving teethmarks on your tongue, if you want to save your relationships with your mate, children, friends, and co-workers, stop being everybody's Mom.

Monitor your Mom-isms. They don't help others; rather, they destroy others' self-esteem and your freedom. To the extent you feel the need to mother another adult, you will also shoulder his responsibility. If *you* are carrying all the responsibility in a relationship, why should the other person even attempt to carry his own? It's interesting that the Chinese symbols for "attachment" and "mother" when combined spell "poison." When we attach ourselves to the role of mother, usurping others' God-given right to learn from their own mistakes, we poison the relationship between us.

MARTYR/VICTIM

We all know people who play martyr/victim roles, people who go around sighing: "Poor me!"; "If only they had . . ."; "Whatever you want . . . (sigh)"; "I don't care . . . (sigh)"; "It's not important how I feel . . . (sigh)."

We learn these roles. We see our mothers and grandmothers manipulating others with them. The martyr/victim roles are incredibly controlling because they evoke *guilt*.

Victims feel powerless and are ruled by others' actions and judgments. People who play the victim role often *were* victimized in childhood when they *were* helpless. As adults, they still feel powerless in their world, ruled by others' actions and opinions. A perpetual victim never has to take responsibility for her own life because everything that happens is obviously someone else's fault. She's a captive of her reactions, not a captain of her actions.

Grown-up victims fill their lives with impossible "should's" and "have-to's," by which they dwell on their failures and lash themselves alternately with perfectionism and ineffectualness.

Alicia's father died when she was very young. She felt her father had abandoned her. Her mother was unstable and became more so after her husband's death. Alicia took on the role of parent to her mother and, over the years preceding her mother's suicide, felt victimized by her situation. She had "given up" her childhood to her mother's emotional dependency. Alicia believed that no matter how much she loved, those she loved would leave her. She wanted and needed love herself, but, entrenched in the victim role, she married a series of men who either abandoned her emotionally or invaded every corner of her life. Alicia's son victimized her, quite literally, by threats of murder and suicide.

She was trapped in her internal litany: "I'm so helpless. Why don't *they* change?" Until she realizes that she is responsible for re-casting herself in the role of victim, she will continue to allow herself to be invaded. Until she begins to honor her limits and boundaries and stand up for her rights, she will continue to live a helplessly restricted life.

Alicia is a "Yes, but . . ." person, so solidified in her identity as victim that she responds to every positive suggestion with, "Yes, but . . .", and there follows a reason why she can't be free of whatever person or situation is currently victimizing her. If I suggest that it might be good for her self-image, bank account, and marriage to get a different job, she says, "Yes, but there are no jobs," or, "Yes, but I don't have up-to-date skills." When told that it's essential that she have therapy to heal and release her old resentments and thought patterns, she says, "Yes, but it would be so *hard,*" or, "Yes, but there aren't any good therapists." She alone is keeping herself stuck in her unhappy victim's role, with her "Yes, butting."

The only way to get out of the victim role is to choose to get out. Become AWARE of the role you're playing; ACKNOWLEDGE it (very important for a victim, because it entails the crucial step of taking personal responsibility); ACCEPT it; and then CHOOSE to alter it. This choice will probably require the help of a therapist and/or friend who can lovingly expose the expressions of the role and their consequences in your life.

I once had a client who said, "Martyrdom is for emergencies only!" I love that statement for the depth of truth in it: we use martyrdom to get what we want from others, to bludgeon them into submission through guilt. While manipulating others, we martyrs can feel so chaste, noble, long-suffering, and self-righteous. But we can also feel incredibly lonely.

My grandmother was a grand master of martyrdom and victimization. No matter what anyone did for her, it wasn't enough. Being around her was a continuous experience of guilt, and consequently we avoided her as much as possible.

No one feels comfortable listening while a martyr whines about all the ways we're responsible for her health, happiness, and self-esteem, and how we've all failed. By fostering guilt in others the martyr isolates herself and creates the very situation she fears: rejection, loss of love, isolation.

These thoughts and others like them are sure tip-offs that you're playing the martyr: "After all I've done for them!" "I gave him the best years of my life, and now look at what he's given me in return!" "If only the children would call once in awhile."

Margaret, a class-A martyr, told me, "The children never call me . . . (sigh)." (Martyrs sigh a lot.) When I asked if she ever called them, she replied that she didn't, for fear they'd feel she was intruding.

Her kids were in a bind. They were supposed to read Mom's mind, and they were guilty if they didn't. Moreover, they'd spent a lifetime getting wise to her martyrdom, and they didn't particularly care to call her up for yet another load of guilt. So Margaret found herself alone a lot until she learned to take responsibility for asking for what she wanted and needed without punishing others with guilt.

INVALID

This role requires little explanation. Who can invade us if we're in chronically ill health? No one can expect us to give ourselves away. No one can refuse to grant our needs and desires. Being chronically sick is powerful. True, little is expected of you . . . but look at the price you pay! When you're sick, your freedom is severely limited. Adopting the invalid role is in-valid!

BITCH

> *A man can be called ruthless if he bombs a*
> *country to oblivion. A woman can be called*
> *ruthless if she puts you on hold.*
> —Gloria Steinem

Many traditionally-minded men (and women) will label you "bitch" if you're assertive and speak up for yourself. And many women deserve the title because they use bitchiness to relieve their pent-up frustration at giving themselves away and being invaded in various ways. They nag, gripe, use toxic humor to put people down, criticize, and, secretly, weep.

Being bitchy isn't much fun either for the bitchee or the bitcher. Bitchiness is generally the result of unspoken rage. It never works as a long-term solution because it corrodes your own self-esteem and alienates others.

Adrienne used to nag her husband when he came home late, gripe when he didn't do things he'd promised, and grumble about him to her friends. When the couple came in for counseling, she was just as down on herself as on him.

They were locked in a deadly game *with no exit*:

she felt neglected and deserted, so she took on the roles of Mother and Bitch, admonishing, nagging, explaining and raving, crying and raging. He played the role of martyr and penitent little boy, passively agreeing with everything she said, then doing exactly what he wanted.

Adrienne was willing to look at her underlying reasons for adopting the Bitch and Mother roles and to stop them, but her husband wouldn't give up his part of the game, and they ultimately divorced. She's generally happy now, though she remembers her marriage with sadness. She's no longer bitchy, and she loves the experience of taking charge of her life. Her relationships are fun and mutually supportive. Her husband has moved on—to a woman who's even more demanding of him than Adrienne was. Adrienne broke the pattern; he did not.

If you react to frustration by feeling like a powerless little terrier, snarling and ripping at a knotted sock, chances are you're playing the Bitch role. Find out what's frustrating you. How are you allowing yourself to be invaded? Do you feel you've given so much of yourself away there's nothing left? Women who resort to bitchiness generally aren't really mean; they're scared, and they long for honest, mutually independent relationships.

GIRL-WOMAN

Women who play Girl-Woman are afraid, too, but they take the opposite tack from the Bitch role. Girl-Women need to be cared for and protected, fathered, and told what to do. Somewhere along the way these women have made the assumption that they aren't lovable unless they're "less than." They may have received the idea that they're incapable of taking care of themselves from over-protective parents who didn't allow them to make decisions, including mistakes, and who taught them that if they wanted to get through life, they'd better find someone to take care of them.

Beth, a tiny, sweet, pretty woman, was in one of our groups. She talked in a soft little-girl voice and said that her husband didn't "let" her do many things. He wouldn't "let" her have a room in their house in which to paint, although he had both study and hobby rooms of his own. She was very concerned that being in the group would make him angry. I said, "How old are you, Beth?" She replied, "Forty-six." After I asked her the question two more times, she looked up out of lowered eyes and giggled, "Sixteen." She had met her husband when she was 16, and there she had frozen, giving away her adulthood in order to hold his love, or so she believed. She felt invaded, resentful, and fearful. She was afraid that if she grew up, he wouldn't love her anymore.

I saw her just the other day. She speaks in an assured, adult manner, works as an administrator for a retirement facility, and is pursuing a graduate degree in Gerontology, having designed the course of study herself. She's very happy *with* her husband. I asked her how old she was, and she replied proudly, "Forty-eight. *And* my husband likes me better this way!" As it turned out, her husband had felt burdened by her continuous need to be parented, and he welcomed an equal relationship, though not without some resistance during the initial part of her change.

When you look inside yourself, do you find the feelings of a Mother, Victim, Invalid, Bitch, or Girl-

Woman? It can be scary to look honestly at our own behavior, but we can take comfort from the fact that virtually everyone who does it finds many things that need to change.

When *we* change, our relationships also begin to change; after all, a relationship *can't* remain the same when one of the persons involved in it changes. Facing the fear of change and acting in spite of it creates freedom. We can even use the greater fear of remaining in our painful ruts to impel ourselves into action. Frequently, the other people in our lives are relieved when we stop giving ourselves away.

Helmer: *Remember—before all else you are a wife and mother.*

Nora: *I don't believe that anymore. I believe that before all else I am a human being, just as you are.*

—HENRIK IBSEN

CHAPTER 12

Yes! We Do Have Rights!

A BILL OF RIGHTS FOR WOMEN

1. I have the right to be treated with respect.
2. I have the right to have and express my feelings and opinions.
3. I have the right to be listened to and taken seriously.
4. I have the right to set my own priorities.
5. I have the right to say No without feeling guilty.
6. I have the right to ask for what I want and need.
7. I have the right to be different than others expect me to be.
8. I have the right to make my own choices.
9. I have the right to laugh and have fun.
10. I have the right to love and be loved.
11. I have the right to be paid fairly for what I do.
12. I have the right to be happy.

The above list was compiled from long-forgotten sources; the source I *do* remember is my own life. In my journey toward independence, I've struggled with each of these issues.

When you read the list, what's your response? If you can say, "Yes, I believe that—I have those rights in my life now," you can fairly claim to have gone beyond dependency and to have achieved the courage to be yourself.

Do some of the items make you shake your head and say, "You've got to be kidding! I could never feel that way! Even if I did, my family and friends would never honor my feelings!" If so, read on.

It really is true that we teach people how to treat us. Before we can expect to be treated well, we must believe we deserve good treatment. Before we can have our rights respected, we must believe that we have rights.

To convince yourself that you have rights, remind yourself constantly of those rights. Post a copy of the above list, or a list of your own making, in a prominent place in your house and work place, where it'll serve two purposes: it'll remind you what you're working towards, implanting positive ideas in your subconscious mind, and it'll make others aware of what you're striving for.

The very act of reading your rights, or at least seeing them daily, helps you stay AWARE that you have those rights, ACKNOWLEDGE the awareness to others, and ACCEPT the fact of your rights with wholehearted conviction. Once you *know* you have rights, you can begin to teach yourself and others to honor your rights.

Kristy worked full-time, yet her husband and two

sons expected her also to assume full responsibility for the household. She went on strike—not just for a day, or a week, but for three months. She shopped, cooked, and washed for herself but not for her family. Previously, she'd been feeling victimized by her situation and unable to come up with a good solution, so she became increasingly resentful and angry. When she realized, "Yes, I have rights, too!" and went on strike, the angry feelings disappeared.

Kristy was willing to risk her family's displeasure. At first, she took a lot of flak. Her husband and sons teased and humored her, thinking she was kidding; by the second week they were furious because they could see how much they'd been demanding, and they knew they were going to have to change. Her strike succeeded; Kristy now has three willing co-workers.

Risk: Taking Responsibility and Making Creative Choices

We must not rely on anyone's saving us, but be very aware of the fact that wrong choices make us incapable of saving ourselves.

—Erich Fromm

Growth, like all forward movement, requires an element of risk, of courting the unexpected. Risking is scary, but without risk in our lives we are not truly living; we are stagnating.

Each risk we take, each pain we heal, each inner dragon we tame widens the path to freedom for others to follow. I like to think of those women who were brave enough to demand the vote and the right to keep property when they married. They broke a trail in consciousness for the rest of us just as surely as the pioneers broke trails to the West.

This new path of consciousness has a few visible, historic landmarks, but for the most part it is an invisible trail, *felt* more than seen. It has been built and paved by the courage, hopes, tears, and fears of the women who've gone before us. Every risk *we* take makes it easier for others to summon the courage to risk being themselves. By creating new patterns for our own actions, we create patterns of loving respect for the rights of all, both women and men.

> *It is not easy to find happiness in ourselves, and it is impossible to find it elsewhere.*
> —Agnes Repplier

Your life is no one's responsibility but your own. There are many things in your life over which you have no control and for which you aren't responsible—but you *are* responsible for how you *respond* to any circumstance. And your response alone determines whether any circumstance becomes resolved for good or ill in your life.

When you become "response-able"—that is, when you learn to choose your responses creatively and consciously—you'll be free to build a life of continued growth and increasing happiness.

For those circumstances in life over which you can't possibly have any control, such as emotional hurts received in early childhood, you can learn to take responsibility for your need to grieve and make creative choices regarding how you will do so.

Victoria, about whom I spoke earlier, was the victim of violent sexual abuse from infancy until 18 years of age. She was not responsible for that early pain, but she is responsible for her response and rehabilitation. Victoria *must* grieve; at this point her pain is so great that she simply has no choice. But she is free to choose *how* she will grieve. Although her struggle is a mighty one, she is risking by experiencing her pain, taking responsibility for her healing, and making creative choices. She is also reaching out to others with similar pain . . . a sure sign of loving healing.

Few of us, thank God, have such deep wounds but all of us bear scars that affect how we lead our lives. We need to take responsibility for treating those old wounds and to choose how we will work to heal them, so that we can move on to better things. Ask yourself: "If I took responsibility for this situation in my life and my response to it, how could I alter, heal, avoid, solve, stop, work with, change it?" If you started counting on yourself for solutions, where would you start?

What's the first, tiny baby step that you'll take? Don't worry about the overall dimensions of the process; just take that one small step. If you need moral support, talk with a friend or professional counselor. But do it!

If you persist in thinking that "they" need to change before you can be happy, you'll never get anywhere. Whether "they" is a mate, friend, the economy, the weather, a circumstance, or unloving parents, if you rely on them to change your life for you—good luck! You're stuck! When you realize that *you're* responsible—not to blame, but responsible—for your own life and happiness, you'll begin building the inner power to change and make creative choices. If, for example, your husband is an alcoholic, you have a choice: either blame the situation and be a victim, or go to Al Anon or take some other practical step toward healing the situation.

Feeling dull and lifeless? What dragon inside you is keeping your sparkle from shining through to the surface? Choose to take responsibility for a healing: explore your life patterns and find out what's going on. Review the four quadrants of your being: physical, emotional, mental, and spiritual. Do you have something going for you in each of these areas, or have you become unbalanced? Is your brain too idle? Take a class in a subject that interests you. Is your body fit and healthy? If not, start eating right and risk exercising even if you look lumpy in tights. Need a good cry? Well, why not? Do it! Want a raise? Ask! Do you feel inwardly at peace? Start taking a few minutes every day for quiet, prayer, and reflection.

Get up 20 minutes earlier to give yourself time for self-improvement activities. Find ways to infuse yourself with enthusiasm. You cannot feel bored, dull, or lifeless and enthusiastic at the same time.

Every change risks a crisis. As you start changing your responses to circumstances, you'll undoubtedly upset some of the people in your life. People resist change, and people are used to you the way you are. The Chinese character for "Crisis" is a combination of the characters for "Danger" and "Opportunity."

DANGER   OPPORTUNITY

As you risk change, you'll create danger to the status quo, but you'll open up new, freeing opportunities for yourself, your family, and your friends. Risk may be scary, but it brings tremendous rewards. Go for it!

It's *your* life; don't waste it. Use the Triple A map to chart a path to a better, happier life. Become AWARE of what needs to change; ACKNOWLEDGE what you want to change; and ACCEPT the fact that *you* are responsible and can choose a course of action. The creative choices you make will change your life for the better.

> *It is not because things are difficult that*
> *we do not dare; it is because we do not dare*
> *that they are difficult.*
>
> —Seneca

Speaking Out Without Blowing Up

> *I was angry with my friend;*
> *I told my wrath, my wrath did end.*
> *I was angry with my foe;*
> *I told it not, my wrath did grow.*
>
> —William Blake

Learning to speak up for yourself is extremely important as you choose risky new actions that threaten the status quo for others. There are two ways to "tell our wrath": the constructive and destructive. We've all seen (and probably done) the destructive method, hiding feelings or blowing our tops and spewing out raw emotions in people's faces. The destructive way causes our wrath and the wrath of others to grow, rather than to go.

How can we speak out without blowing up or causing others to blow up?

First, convince yourself that you have the right to speak out. If you need to refresh your memory, refer to the Bill of Rights listed earlier. You may also want to search your consciousness for seed sentences that are preventing others from hearing and respecting your words. One of mine used to be: "If you don't have anything nice to say, don't say anything at all."

I surrounded myself with friends who'd been trained, as I had, to be afraid of confrontation and honest communication. When I spoke my feelings, my friends told me that what I had to say wasn't "nice," and I believed them. So for years I stuffed my feelings back inside even when I needed to share them, fearing I'd be rejected, labeled a bitch, or rock the boat of my precarious emotional dependence.

Once you believe you have a right to voice your feelings and opinions, you'll need to learn *how* to speak out constructively. Speaking out in order to make others see the issue our way, to convince them, or to prove them wrong is acting destructively. We need to learn to speak out with the goal of *understanding* each other: speaking without blaming, and listening without judging.

*It takes two to speak the truth—one to
speak, and another to hear.*
                    —Henry David Thoreau

BLOW UP . . . BUT . . .

Blowing up is like taking out the garbage:
our minds create emotional garbage that in turn
creates harmful toxins in our bodies. If we don't
blow up and blow off those toxins, chances are
we'll "blow in" and create such suppression-related
maladies as depression, heart disease, and even
cancer.

Lots of women "blow out"—i.e., get fat. I can always tell when I'm holding something back: I put
on weight.

There's an art to blowing up constructively. When
your inner dragons have built up a good head of
steam, you need to blow it out *so long as you aim it
away from people and breakable objects.* Little children
know innately how to blow up: they fling themselves on the floor and pound and kick. Very rarely
do they hurt themselves.

Wise parents and teachers call "time outs" to allow kids to express themselves. The child can go off
by herself, away from others, and express to her
heart's content. Give yourself time out! Take the
force of your anger and frustration away from people, and let 'er rip. Only *then* speak out.

After taking time out to release excess energy, we
can talk and listen constructively with the help of a
few simple communication tools. I'll talk about
these shortly, but first here are some examples of
constructive blow-ups:

VERBALIZE	Loud is important! Scream on the freeway. Don't say anything nice. Talk naughty! You'll never see those people driving beside you again, and it'll give them something to think about.
HIT	Physical exertion is an especially good channel for anger. Jogging and handball are okay, but physical activity directed specifically at releasing your dragon's fire is best.

The large body bags used by boxers are great. I use an old tennis racket to wallop the bed. Large athletic socks stuffed with rags or other socks and tied at the end are fantastic for hitting and throwing. They make a nice, satisfying sound. Kick a beanbag chair. Throw eggs at trees (birds love raw eggs). Throw rocks into rivers, lakes, the ocean, and throw your anger away with them.

Scribble ferocious pictures on big pieces of paper. Get on the floor and yell and scream as you tear up butcher paper or a phone book.

If you really go for it while you blow up, you'll feel tired but cleansed. Robert Frost said, "The best way out is always through." I believe this is true of the emotions.

Tools for Constructive Communication

*The best impromptu speeches are those
written well in advance.*

—Ruth Gordon

A. PREPARE FOR COMMUNICATION BY:

1. Blowing up privately.
2. Clarifying what you're feeling and what you
   want to say:
   • Make notes to yourself. A client of mine
     takes an emotional memo to herself, labeled
     "Memo to Me . . . I'm angry about
     (_____)!" She writes down her
     feelings and puts them in the "IN" basket to be
     worked out at a more convenient time. *Always*
     come back to those "IN" files, if only to see if
     your feelings are now clear. If you don't check
     back, it's a sign you're wanting to suppress
     those feelings.
   • Organize what you want to communicate.
   • Rehearse.

Remember, communication isn't guerilla warfare.
The reason for speaking out is to create *love, understanding,* and *intimacy.*

B. TIMING

I can't stress enough how important timing is to
good communication! It's essential! Many people

ruin any chance for constructive communication by choosing the wrong time to speak. Those four little words, "We need to talk," strike terror in the hearts of people who aren't *ready* to talk. If we add "Now!", we're setting ourselves up to be met defensively. It is an absolute "must" that both parties agree willingly on a time to talk.

In our family, we've evolved a system that works for us. If I want to talk to my husband, I'll tell him I need to talk sometime within the next 24 hours. I tell him the subject—*briefly*, limiting myself to one or two sentences, maximum. Then I let him know just how big a deal it is for me. Since he can choose the time, which needs to be mutually agreeable, he has a sense of participating in the process. If I were to jump on him and demand that we talk "right now", he'd feel attacked and defensive.

When he chooses the time, he can muster his thoughts on the subject—he can prepare. Some people find it helps to make regular appointments to "clear the boards." They'll have dinner once a week or perhaps schedule 10 or 20 minutes each evening to talk.

C. COMMUNICATING

1. *Re-state your goal.* Before you start talking, take a few deep breaths, hold hands, and each state your goal for the discussion. What do you hope to gain? Learn? Understand? If you stray from the subject, remind each other.
2. *State how you feel.* As you begin the discussion, what are your fears and physical symptoms? Instead of protecting yourself behind masks of attack, indifference, or bravado, show your vulnerabilities. When I need to talk about some-

thing uncomfortable, my body gets very anxious. So I might say, "This is really hard for me. My heart is racing and my stomach is churning. I'm perspiring and my tongue feels as big and dry as a throw rug."

3. *Check Your Reality*. Sometimes what we feel is coming from the other person isn't what was intended. Before you react, check out your assumptions: "I need a reality check. I feel shut out. Are you angry with me?" If the answer is yes, you can choose to pursue it now or later. If the answer is no, accept it. If your feeling persists, check it out again.

4. *Use "I Messages"*. These tend to eliminate defensiveness.

The formula is:
"When you do/say (_____),
I feel (_____)."

The idea is to express *real feelings*, not judgments or accusations. Use one or two words at most to describe a real feeling. Examples of feelings: "hurt," "confused," "tired," "angry," "joyful," "uncomfortable," "abandoned," "excited." Feelings describe what's happening to *you*, rather than a judgment about whatever the other person is doing. Here's an example of a clear "I Message": "When you talk to me in that tone of voice, I feel hurt and angry."

By contrast, "You Messages" point fingers, make judgments, criticize personally, and interpret. The "I Message" above could have been sent as a "You Message": "When you talk to me in that tone of voice, you're doing it just to hurt me!" or, "You make me feel awful. You hurt me!" The silent tag line at the end of a "You Message" is, "You bastard, you!"

"I Messages" *inform*. "You Messages" *attack*.

EXAMPLES:

You Messages	I Messages
You are disgusting and irresponsible when you drink.	When you drink, I feel scared and disgusted.
You are rude and irresponsible not to call when you are going to be late.	I feel like an abandoned kid when you don't call if you are going to be late.
You are an insensitive bully to tease me when you know it hurts me.	When you tease me, I feel helpless and angry.

D. NON-VERBAL COMMUNICATION

One of my clients was in the hospital after the birth of her son. Her mother-in-law visited her and said, "I saw you had a lot of flowers yesterday, so I brought you something today." She handed her a small, unwrapped cactus still boasting its Safeway 79-cent price tag. A great non-verbal put-down.

Actions speak louder than words. When our non-verbal messages are out of sync with our words, everyone gets confused. We've all had the experience of being in the presence of someone who was acting so cold that your nose hairs froze, yet when asked what was wrong s/he said (frostily), "Nothing!" That's a mixed (or "double") message.

E. LISTENING

Listening is probably *the* most important part of any communication. Listening leads to understanding and creates a bridge to intimacy.

1. *Allow Pauses.* Before you formulate a response, be sure you've taken time to really *hear* what your partner says. Resist the tendency to race ahead of your partner's thoughts, stacking up "retort ammunition." Really *listen!*

   Silent pauses are an essential feature of real communication. If you keep trying to break in while the other person is talking, you are *not* listening. People can't communicate unless you affirm their worth by allowing them to be *really* heard. Understanding requires hearing. Relationships thrive on understanding. If you want to have successful relationships, *listen.*

2. *Reflect Back* what you believe your partner has just said. If you've ever played the parlor game of Gossip (also called Telephone), where a message gets passed by one person whispering it to the next around a circle, you know that messages get easily distorted by being mis-heard. Ask if you've heard correctly. Make sure you're both talking about the same issue or feeling. Don't assume you "know" what's meant. You know what they

say about "assume": it makes an "ass" out of "u" and "me."

Reflect. Explore. Make sure you understand. To really listen takes patience and desire. The rewards are well worth it!

Honoring What We Want and Need

Why do women leave home to take their services into the marketplace? Money? For sure.

But maybe they felt the need to materialize. You had to have been there to know what it was like to be invisible. To move and not be seen, to talk and not be heard. To have family return to the house every evening and say, "Anyone home?"

—Erma Bombeck

Have you ever felt invisible? Who alone of all the people you know has the power to make you visible? You! And you'll never be visible unless you honor your wants and needs.

What is it you want and need? Affection? Approval? Love? Hugs? To be heard? To succeed? To have help around the house? Do you ask for help filling those wants and needs—or do you hope people will psychically "know" about them without your asking? That's not fair. Expecting people to read your mind hardly *ever* gets you what you need.

Simone, a school teacher, was going through her second divorce and feeling bereft and worthless. Finally, she worked up the courage to ask for what she needed: lots of hugs, and acknowledgement that she was okay even though twice divorced. She made a badge, which she wore at school. It said: "I need eight hugs a day!" Her willingness to ask for what she wanted sparked a revolution at her school. Soon people were not only hugging her but hugging others as well. A climate of closeness developed among the staff which hadn't existed in the "pre-hug" days.

Other people can never give us *all* that we want and need, so we must learn to fill our own wants and needs also.

Pat is newly single, and she needs love and hugs. Her underlying need for affection had its origins in a nonsupportive relationship with her mother, and the separation from her husband only exacerbated it. Pat's inner little girl is crying for loving acceptance.

I keep a doll in my office, and when I gave it to Pat to hold, she poured out to it all the love that *her* inner child craves. I encouraged her to buy herself a doll or teddy bear. Silly as it sounds, it helps. Hugging, holding, talking to an accepting cuddly toy encourages us to develop gentle, healing attitudes toward our inner child. You might try hugging several bears or dolls in the store until you find one that feels just right to you.

Pat's case is a good example of how external objects can help us to explore our inner wants and needs and to honor them. You have a right to know your own needs and fulfill them. Explore ways to ask for what you need or to fill your needs for yourself.

As you gain confidence in your rights and learn to honor your wants and needs, you'll open doors to inner wholeness and health. You'll move beyond dependence and discover the courage to be yourself. You'll discover your own excellence and encourage others to discover theirs.

Part Five

Healing:
Owning Your Own
Excellence

*We must overcome the notion
that we must be regular . . .
It robs you of the chance
to be extraordinary
and leads you to the mediocre.*

—UTA HAGEN

Healing: Owning Your Own Excellence

IT'S ONLY RECENTLY that self-esteem has become a household world. We now help our children to develop it, and we try to enhance it in ourselves. But when I was growing up, self-esteem was hard to come by. People confused it with self-centeredness and big-headedness.

One of my early fears was that I would appear conceited and people wouldn't like me. So I played down my talents with a kind of bogus humility. Most of the parents I knew had low self-esteem, so we children had few models to show us what real self-esteem looked—or felt—like.

If parents don't balance their criticisms with appreciation for things done well or for our willingness to learn, we grow up to be critical of ourselves and others. Self-critical people see their own mistakes leaping about before them festooned with neon lights, while their triumphs wither from lack of attention. They look at their real or imagined shortcomings with powerful binoculars and look at their good points and successes through the wrong end of the binoculars. Failures loom large, and successes look like specks on the horizon—mere accidents of nature.

I used to have a deadly eye for the positives in myself and a caressing eye for the negatives. Do you ever dwell painfully on something dumb you've said? I did that all the time. I'd even go back over encounters with people, *looking* for things I'd said wrong. One of my seed sentences was: "You always put your foot in your mouth!" I mentally scanned every encounter for the taste of shoe leather.

It never occurred to me to go back over a meeting with someone and *congratulate* myself for something I had said *well*. Now, I do that frequently because I've discovered that it is possible to cultivate our own excellence. It's a matter of retraining yourself to behave like a loving parent toward yourself, encouraging your good points and consoling yourself gently when you fail.

Give yourself permission to know what a fantastic person you are! Learn to "SEE": *Savor Excellence Everyday.* Start liking and admiring yourself, loving and nurturing yourself. Become an honest *and* appreciative mirror for yourself.

Self-esteem is quiet and confident; it doesn't need boasting and self-centeredness. True self-esteem empowers you to be loving and giving. Realize that you needn't fear you'll become selfish if you honor your excellence. Actually, you will en-

courage others to accept their excellence as you accept your own.

Gold Star List

When I was still learning to be more kind and
friendly toward myself, I made "gold star lists." Before going to sleep every night I made a list of at
least a half-dozen things I'd said, done, or felt during the day that deserved a gold star. This worked
so well for me that I now ask my clients who have
low self-esteem to make similar lists of their star-
worthy actions and qualities. It teaches them to fo-
cus on their positive qualities.

Rate your actions relatively: for example, on a
day when you're feeling lousy or you're ill, give
yourself a gold star just for getting out of bed and
brushing your teeth. Be a little creative and outra-
geous: your list doesn't have to be all goody-two-
shoes items. I recently gave myself permission to
have a rip-roaring *constructive* temper tantrum. I had
been building up a lot of frustration and grief, so I
beat up on my office couch with a stuffed sock,
screamed, and had a good cry. Then I gave myself
three stars, one for having the temper tantrum, one
for not directing it *at* anybody, and one for not feeling guilty about it afterward.

The kinds of actions you put on your list will be
unique to you, depending on where you are on the
road to self-esteem. It might include such statements as: "I didn't call myself stupid all day." Buy
yourself a packet of gold stars and *do it*! It's fun, and
it's an A-plus way to start an attitude change. It'll
help you turn your powerful mind into a friend

instead of an enemy. Learn to re-focus your attention on your good actions and qualities—you *do* have excellence already.

Becoming aware of your good points is one of the most powerful steps you can take toward developing the courage to be yourself.

*Who knows what women can be
when they are finally free to become themselves?
Who knows what women's
intelligence will contribute
when it can be nourished without denying love?*

—BETTY FRIEDAN

CHAPTER 13

Having The Courage

Give Yourself Permission

Sometimes, all it takes to make great strides toward having the courage to be yourself is giving yourself permission. Too often, we wait around for someone to tell us it's okay. But ask yourself: is there anybody in your life who *really* has that kind of power over you? No! No one else can give you the go-ahead to change. No one else knows the inner longings, dreams, *and* fears that struggle within you. Thus, only *you* can know where and how you should give yourself permission to become authentically yourself.

Growth and unfoldment begin when we give ourselves permission to *Be*. Remember this sentence from the Bill of Rights (see Chapter 12): "I have the right to be different than others expect me to be."

These words are written on the tomb of an Anglican bishop who was buried in the crypts of Westminster Abbey in 1100 AD:

> When I was young and free and my imagination had no limits, I dreamed of changing the world.
>
> As I grew older and wiser, I discovered the world would not change, so I shortened my sights somewhat and decided to change only my country.
>
> But it too seemed immovable.
>
> As I grew into my twilight years, in one last desperate attempt, I settled for changing only my family, those closest to me, but alas, they would have none of it.
>
> And now as I lie on my deathbed, I suddenly realize:
>
> If I had only changed myself first, then by example I might have changed my family.
>
> From their inspiration and encouragement I would then have been able to better my country, and who knows,
>
> I may have even changed the world.

Nobody Said It Would Be Easy

Courage, as this book defines it, is the willingness to act even when frightened. If we've been emotionally dependent on others for a long time, it will be frightening to make independent decisions about our lives. The only way to begin is to take steps that you *can* handle. Even a baby step puts you further forward than no step at all. You'll be quite surprised at how much strength, confidence, and pride you get from tapping just a little bit of your hidden inner courage.

Put a 3 x 5 card on your fridge, mirror, or in your wallet that says:

> ## NOBODY SAID
> ## IT WOULD BE
> ## EASY!

Too often, we hold the underlying assumption that things *should* be easy, that if we face difficult challenges, it means that we're somehow bad, or the world is against us. With that victim attitude, you'll find it all too easy to crumble and never discover how strong and creative you really can be. Change *isn't* easy—ever. Avoiding the difficulties in our lives, we never conquer fear. When we face challenges and win, or when we overcome a fear, we experience wonderful feelings of accomplishment and mastery.

Resistance Magnifies Pain

That the yielding conquers the resistant and the soft conquers the hard is a fact known by all persons, yet utilized by none. . . .

—Lao Tzu

Get rid of the attitude that things "should" be easy, which only encourages you to resist difficulties. Shun the "ain't it awful" and "woe is me" attitudes in yourself and in other people. Negativity is *highly* contagious, so if at all possible, avoid being around chronically negative people.

Natural childbirth classes teach mothers-to-be that the pain of childbirth is greater when you resist it and grow tense with fear. They tell you to "breathe into the pain"—not because deep breathing decreases the pain, but because relaxation increases your ability to accept pain.

In my bereavement groups I meet many people who try to resist their pain. I encourage them to "lean into" it, to relax into the experience of pain, to give themselves permission to feel it and act on it. This frequently amazes them because most of them have been taught the stiff-upper-lip approach to pain.

Resistance magnifies! The more we resist people or circumstances, the more we draw to us exactly that which we resist. Perhaps that's what Jesus meant when he spoke of turning the other cheek. Resistance causes tension. Tension creates tightness, stiffness, inflexibility, and being stiff, tight, and inflexible makes you vulnerable. In a wind storm, the heavy oak tree resists and the willow yields. The willow, which doesn't stand stolidly in the path of the wind but rather allows it to whip through its branches, clearly has the better chance of surviving.

Remember this formula:
Resistance→Tension→Inflexibility→Vulnerability.

When you feel yourself resisting (tension will be the first sign), become AWARE of what or whom you're resisting. What circumstances, memories, attitudes, or relationships are threatening you with pain? Are you magnifying the pain by resisting?

ACKNOWLEDGE what you discover about your patterns of resistance. Finally, ACCEPT that the source of pain exists and that you're feeling resistance to it. Then CHOOSE to let it be and to act appropriately.

Remember: resistance is blind reaction, not free choice. You become free when you can choose how you will act.

Resistance can also signal the presence of a power struggle: a desire to be right, to prove a point, to be in control. The only way to win a power struggle is to give it up. Resistance to other people's opinions and feelings is just as useless as resistance to our own. Your pain or discomfort is magnified in direct proportion to your resistance. When your husband is cranky and you think he "shouldn't" be and you resist his mood, you'll feel worse and very likely provoke him further by your resistance. You don't have to stick around and bear the brunt of his mood. Only he can change it, so why resist?

Sylvia hated her husband's constant put-downs about her weight and the fact that he rarely told her he loved her. She entered into the spirit of a power struggle, pointing out every small proof that he was wrong and unloving. In her resisting mood, she didn't see any of the loving things he did. They became like two boxers, jabbing the air in their respective corners in anticipation of the next round. Both were in pain.

As she became aware of the destructive path they both were taking, Sylvia gradually stopped resisting. She didn't give up her rights, but she got off her husband's back. She became more flexible, able to express her real feelings instead of lashing out emotionally in revenge. She stated her wants and needs, but not in an accusing, judging way. When he couldn't give her what she needed, she became creative at filling her needs herself. She stopped resisting him and chose instead to make a better life for herself, not out of resentment but out of love for herself.

As Sylvia gained independence, she began to feel less like her husband's victim and increasingly able to reach out to him with love. He'd been resisting her demands for love and affection, but as she demanded less, he felt more like giving.

Kahlil Gibran writes:

> Your pain is the breaking of the shell that encloses your understanding.
> Even as the stone of the fruit must break, that its heart may stand in the sun, so must you know pain.
> And could you keep your heart in wonder at the daily miracles of your life, your pain would not seem less wondrous than your joy;
> And you would accept the seasons of your heart, even as you have always accepted the seasons that pass over your fields.
> And you would watch with serenity through the winters of your grief.

Give Yourself Credit

Remember, Ginger Rogers did everything
Fred Astaire did, but she did it backward
and in high heels.
—Faith Whittlesey

If your life were a bank, how many daily deposits and withdrawals would you make to and from the accounts of your body, feelings, mind, and spirit? In fact, we *do* have a "life account," from which we frequently make too many withdrawals or allow others to withdraw too freely. We need to credit our lives liberally and debit sparingly in order to have a comfortable "balance." When we overdraw physically, emotionally, mentally and spiritually, we "see red"—i.e., we experience frustration and anger.

EMOTIONAL BANK ACCOUNT

Debits:
- Unhealed wounds
- Self-condemnation
- Overwork
- Judgment
- Perfectionism
- Isolation
- Unreasonable expectations
- Resistance

A negative life-balance, caused by too many debits, leads to emotional overdrafts such as these:

- Low self-esteem
- Overweight
- Emotional dependence
- Unhappiness
- Depression
- Exhaustion
- Apathy
- Illness

Credits:
- Setting limits
- Self-acceptance
- Exercise
- Listening to yourself
- Healing old wounds
- Friends
- Solitude
- Loving

Credits, which create a positive life balance, lead to emotional surpluses such as:

- High self-esteem
- Energy
- Self-confidence
- Courage
- Authenticity
- Joy
- Healing
- Fulfilling relationships

Debit and Credit Examples

DEBIT	CREDIT
"How stupid can you be?"	"Everyone makes mistakes, I'll do better next time."
"Yes" (when you mean "no")	"No, I'm sorry. I can't do _____."
Feeling guilty	Apologizing for real slights and mistakes.
"Everything's just fine." (false smile)	Being truthful about your feelings.
"No, I don't need a thing."	"What I could use is a good hug!"
"I never do as well as who's-it."	"Great! I did that better than before."
You Messages (saying things you'll regret)	I Messages (not "gunny-sacking")
Over-scheduling and rushing	Realistic goals and schedules
No time for yourself	Relaxing: taking time to smell the flowers
Over-sitting; lots of TV	Exercise
Concentrating on your failures	Celebrating your successes

You alone are in charge of your emotional bank account. Other people should be allowed to withdraw from your account *only* if you give them permission to.

Be liberal with your deposits and extremely frugal with your withdrawals. *Never* write a blank check!

Nourishing from Overflow

We nourish best from overflow.

—Moi'

An important part of owning our own excellence is nourishing ourselves and others and doing so in the best way possible: by *giving* love and support, rather than bartering it. We need to build up an ample surplus in our life account in order to have an overflow from which we can give freely, without expectations and strings attached.

As a measure of the balance in your life account—how well you're taking care of yourself—make a calendar like the one following:

DAY	1	2	3	4	5	6	7
PHYSICAL							
EMOTIONAL							
MENTAL							
SPIRITUAL							

Make a note *every day* of what you've done for yourself in each of the four areas. Keep an eye out for areas that need attention. Ask yourself if you're leading a balanced life.

Much of our lives today is spent in the mental and physical areas, while our emotional and spiritual quadrants wither. Make a commitment to invest energy in all four areas. Slowly, gently make adjustments to your daily routine. Add a little exercise or a few quiet minutes alone listening to healing and inspiring music. Be aware of your resistance to change, and don't sabotage yourself by demanding the impossible. Make small changes, build on your successes, and celebrate every change; thus you'll build the positive expectation and energy to change your routine. Soon you'll feel like a different person, with a changed and more interesting life.

Filling up your own life account before you fill others' takes courage because it seems to contradict the old dictum to "think of others before you think of yourself" or "live a life of service and sacrifice." You have little to give when your own life account is dangerously depleted. When you fill your cup so that the overflow spills out to others, you'll be able to give more freely and willingly. People will sense that you're giving from a sense of abundance, so they'll be able to receive without guilt or obligation. You're *giving* to them, not expecting an equal return. We nourish best from *overflow*!

As a matter of fact,
we are always affirming something,
be it for good or ill.
We are always either saying,
"I can" or "I cannot."
What we need to do is to eliminate the negative
and accentuate the positive.
In doing this we shall gradually acquire
the habit of affirmative thinking.

—ERNEST HOLMES

CHAPTER 14

The Power Of Thought

WISE PEOPLE throughout the ages have spoken of the tremendous power of human thought:

Marcus Aurelius:	*"Our life is what our thoughts make it."*
Solomon:	*"As a man thinketh, so is he."*
Buddha:	*"All that we are is the result of what we have thought."*
William James:	*"Belief creates the actual fact."*
Emerson:	*"What a man thinks of himself, that is which determines, or rather indicates, his fate."*
Henry Ford:	*"Whether you think you can or think you can't, you're right."*

Thinking Is the Birth of Feeling

The last of the human freedoms is to choose one's attitude in any given set of circumstances.

—Victor Frankl

We generally keep more than one thought-track going at the same time in our minds. Some are closer to the surface of consciousness than others. But we are constantly talking to ourselves. This is called *"self talk."*

Listen to what you're saying to yourself in the privacy of your own mind. If what you habitually tell yourself is optimistic, uplifting, and loving, you're certain to be a person who feels happy and energized. If the tone of your thoughts is self-recriminating, resistant, or negative, you'll inevitably feel down and depressed. Thought is the birth of feeling.

Negative, fearful self-talk debits your emotional bank account and buys painful feelings. One of the quickest ways to put yourself in a bad mood is to let yourself worry about the future. I call this *"falling in the future hole."* Future Hole self-talk statements can begin with: "What if . . .," "I couldn't handle . . .," "I'm afraid that . . ."

Our minds, if undisciplined, wander off easily from the here and now into projections of the future. We need to *plan* for the future but not worry. Planning causes secure feelings; worry causes pain. Planning is empowering; worry is victimizing.

Check your self-talk: how do you speak to yourself? Are you kind and encouraging? Would you talk similarly to a close friend? How are your thoughts contributing to your feelings? In positive ways or negative ways? It isn't circumstance that creates our feelings; it's our *thoughts* about circumstances which give birth to our feelings.

Carrie had been unhappy in her marriage for a long time. She often said, "I wish Bill would just leave!" Finally, Bill left, and Carrie fell apart. In her fear and grief at being alone, she forgot how unhappy they had been together. Now she could only see how awful she felt that he was gone. She couldn't handle being abandoned, and she blamed herself totally. Her pain, which was natural, was increased by her self-talk.

The circumstance Carrie had in fact desired was now made unbearable by what she was telling herself about it. Her resistance was magnifying her pain.

Carrie could have alleviated and healed her pain by becoming aware of her victimizing self-talk and choosing to replace it with supportive positive affirmations. For example, every time she found herself repeating the old, painful litany, she could have said, "I am strong and able to handle all circumstances that come my way!"

Your feelings, and the thoughts that created them, are your own responsibility, nobody else's. Take responsibility (not blame!) for changing your thoughts if you want to change your feelings. When you choose to change your thoughts, you cease to be a victim. As your thoughts and feelings become more positive, supportive, and life-affirming, your experience of life will be freer. You'll be encouraged to be yourself.

What You Think You Are, You Will Become

The unleashed power of the atom has changed everything except our modes of thinking, and we thus drift toward unparalleled catastrophes.

—Albert Einstein

Imagine your mind as a garden. Which thoughts will you plant in it? Negative, unhealthy, self-critical thoughts are like weeds. When you plant positive, healthy thoughts, you can expect a crop of beautiful flowers. Thus you alone determine whether your life looks like an overgrown weed-patch or a well-tended, lushly beautiful flower garden.

If you've allowed your mind to drift along as it pleases for a long time (and most of us have), you'll need to train yourself gradually to be a healthy thinker. Tune in without judgment to what you are thinking. If your thinking isn't leading your life toward healthy attitudes and positive feelings, change the channel.

Changing your thoughts is simple; which is not to say it's *easy*. No habit is easy to break, and unhealthy thinking is one of the most stubborn habits of all, one we may have built up over a lifetime. Have faith, though: what you've done, you can—patiently—undo. It will take practice and perseverance, but believe me, it is worth the challenge!

Very simply, you CHOOSE to change your thinking, and then you formulate a plan of action. Here's an example from my life:

When I started to write this book, it became very

clear to me that I was running full-speed into my fears of failure. In school I had always dreaded writing themes and essays, and the thought of writing a *book* terrified me. On the day I was to meet the literary agent for the first time, I used hair spray instead of deodorant and lost my car in the parking lot where I'd parked for two years. I was completely spaced out, and no wonder. At the time, my dominant self-talk was: "What in the world do you think you're doing! You can't write! You got C's in English (I hadn't, but I felt as if I had.) You must be crazy! *You* don't have anything to say."

My mind was full of extremely unhealthy self-talk—in fact, my mind had become my enemy. I felt anxious and disoriented. I decided to change my thoughts. I tentatively assured myself that I *did* have something to say. After all, I had spent years as a working therapist and had achieved a great deal, using the ideas I proposed to write about. I began to feel less anxious . . . or so I thought.

As I mentioned earlier, I arrived at my office for my first scheduled writing marathon without my research files, notes, tape recorder, and very important tapes. All of this stuff—my book!—was scattered all over the road, since I had left it on top of the car when I drove off.

Why was I sabotaging myself? I realized I was afraid that if I failed, I'd look stupid, and I'd have wasted a lot of time. If I succeeded, people might be jealous, and I still had a lot of memories about high school and family issues concerning jealousy. Could an "ordinary" girl like me do something "exceptional"—like becoming an author?

I never realized until lately that women
were supposed to be the inferior sex.
                    —Katherine Hepburn

Unlike Miss Hepburn, I *had* realized we were supposed to be inferior! The book was pushing me out of my comfort zone, across limits beyond which I couldn't very well continue to function if I felt inferior. I was going to have to *risk*.

I began to take the project more lightly. Someone once said, *"Angels fly because they take themselves lightly."* I had been taking writing so seriously I could hardly walk, let alone fly. I decided to **SOAR:** **S**tretch **O**ut **A**nd **R**isk. I decided I would enjoy the writing while I did it and have fun being an author. Having chosen to think differently, I began to put into effect some well-chosen positive affirmations.

Become a Healthy Thinker

The select few who've mastered the art of meditation can empty their minds; the rest of us can't stop thinking, and much of what we think isn't at all conducive to happiness. Therefore, when we catch ourselves thinking negatively, we need to *plan* a script of thoughts to replace our unhealthy self-talk.

Avoid the error of chastising yourself for negative thinking. If you catch yourself in the middle of some particularly insidious negative self-talk and berate yourself ("There I go again! Old gutter-brain! Why *can't* I stop this?"), you'll only start a new pile of negative, self-critical thoughts. Instead, give yourself a gold star for a good job of vigilant thought-monitoring.

I watch my self-talk carefully. I was recently working with a client who's suicidal. After the session I noticed I was feeling depressed, on the verge of tears. I tuned in to my self-talk: I'd been saying, "I should be able to save her! If she dies, I'll be responsible. I can't stand it if she doesn't get well!" No wonder I felt lousy.

I checked the reality of those debilitating thoughts and began to replace them with, "She is a child of God, safe in the universe. I am a good therapist. I love myself and her." I pictured her well and happy. I began to feel better. Sad, still, but then it was a sad situation. But I changed the statements that were giving me pain and began to release my feelings of failure and fear, feelings which would have become obstacles to my helping her.

Affirmations are flower seeds that we plant in our subconscious. They have a powerful effect in helping us build a life that is happy, creative, and free from fear. Conscious affirmations are an effective means of re-programming negative self-talk, underlying assumptions, and hidden attitudes.

Probably the most important affirmation you can have is: "I love myself." If you simply can't say that, try "I am willing to love myself," or, "I am willing to be willing to love myself." Whenever you become aware of unhealthy self-talk, replace it with one of the following affirmations, or create your own affirmations to meet your particular needs:

Positive Self-Talk Affirmations

1. I love myself.
2. I am a good friend to myself and others.
3. I am a creative and worthwhile person even though I make mistakes.
4. Money is flowing to me in ever-increasing amounts.
5. I know my limits and boundaries and stand up for them in a firm and loving manner.
6. I now have time, energy, wisdom, and money to accomplish all that I desire.
7. I am powerful in my life.
8. I am now willing to be my ideal weight and have my ideal appearance.
9. I am a valuable and important person, and I am worthy of the love and respect of others.
10. I have satisfying and supportive relationships.
11. I feel creative and valued in my work.
12. Every day in every way I am getting better and better.

YOUR OWN AFFIRMATIONS: FLOWER SEED SENTENCES

To be effective, affirmations need to be in the present tense. Write your affirmations as if they were true *now*:

1. _____
2. _____
3. _____
4. _____
5. _____
Etc. _____

We not only become what we think; we become what we picture and feel. While repeating them, picture the realities behind your affirmations as clearly and in as much detail as possible. If you're affirming that you're a worthwhile person, close your eyes and see or sense a picture of yourself being appreciated by others—or look in the mirror and tell yourself eye-to-eye how valuable and worthwhile you are. If you receive a note or card of appreciation, carry it with you and look at it often.

Don't expect quick results. You are reprogramming your subconscious mind—the most complex computer on earth. It will take time for your feelings to catch up with your new thoughts. But even if you don't feel the truth of the affirmation now, know that *real work is being done* in the subconscious. This has been proven true over and over again by people who faithfully, persistently practice the science of affirmations. These include world-class athletes and successful business people.

Think of the process of re-programming your self-talk as being similar to training a puppy to the leash. At first, the puppy digs in its paws, puts its head down, and refuses to walk. Once it gets used to the idea, it runs ahead eagerly, enjoying the experience. Our feelings are quite similar: once our self-talk becomes self-loving and healthy, we will surge ahead, freer and happier.

You may hear an insidious internal voice, sneering at your efforts and discounting any possibility of this dumb exercise working. It'll tell you you're bound to fail. It'll try to make you feel hopeless and helpless. It'll negate your right to be happy. It'll tell you that affirmations are too simple to be "scientific."

The following exercise is a good one for exorcising the internal Discounter who stands over our shoulder and says, "Oh yeah!?! Wanna bet!? Not on your life!"

Take a blank sheet of paper and *print* carefully in the left column your affirmation; then in the right column quickly *write* any negative response from the Discounter. Continue carefully *printing* the *same affirmation* in the left column and quickly dashing off all negative comments in the right column until you've exhausted the Discounter. Now you are ready to use your affirmation unhindered by your own inner saboteur.

Self-Talk Discounter Exorcism

AFFIRMATION *(print carefully)*	NEGATIVE RESPONSES *(write quickly)*
1. I love myself.	You've got to be kidding.
2. I love myself.	Why? No one else does!
3. I love myself.	You don't deserve love!
4. I love myself.	You've done a lot of awful things.
5. I love myself.	You aren't a good Christian.
6. I love myself.	Maybe a little, sometimes.
7. I love myself.	But you're 20 pounds overweight! You'll be lovable when you lose them.

8. I love myself.	You make so many mis-takes . . . but you try hard.
9. I love myself.	I'm tired of writing this.
10. I love myself.	Okay, okay . . .
11. I love myself.	I do love myself . . . yes, I deserve love.

Use your affirmations faithfully. CHOOSE how you will think. Picture yourself already experiencing the circumstances or attitudes you're affirming. You'll begin to experience the freedom of being yourself.

> *Your mind is a sacred enclosure into which nothing harmful can enter except by your permission.*
>
> —Arnold Bennett

You are in charge of what enters your mind. When worries plague you, put them on what my dad calls his "2:00 a.m. Worrying List." Being a very sound sleeper, he rarely gets to that list.

Read only materials that feed your soul and uplift your thoughts. Be with people who are positive, optimistic, and happy. Find ways to protect yourself from absorbing negative "vibes." Don't subject yourself to negative TV and movie fare. You may feel unaffected, but your subconscious will carry negativity around for days, perhaps even years. It is junk food for the mind.

You can plant thought-seeds of lack, in which case you'll end up believing in and experiencing lack. Or you can plant thought-seeds of plenty. It's up to you: you can believe in your limitations, or you can believe you can soar.

My son is a good example of the power of belief. His lifelong ambition was to be a professional athlete. During his senior year in high school, his right knee was severely injured, and he was told by an orthopedic surgeon that he'd never play sports again, and, furthermore, that there was a good chance he'd walk with a limp for the rest of his life. He and I refused to believe in that limitation, and we searched until we found a knee specialist who gave us hope. Two years and three surgeries later, he completed his first triathlon race: a 1½-mile swim, a 50-mile bike ride, and a 13-mile marathon run. He chose to believe he *could*, and he did! You can too!

As you become a healthy thinker, you are well on the way to becoming a loving and tolerant friend to yourself and to others.

Flowers are lovely: love is flower-like
Friendship is a sheltering tree.

—SAMUEL COLERIDGE

CHAPTER 15

Becoming A Loving And Tolerant Friend To Yourself

IN MANY WAYS throughout this book I've stressed that it's essential to become a loving and tolerant friend to yourself. Do *you* act as a sheltering tree in your own life? Take a moment to think about how you treat your friends. Do you express the same kindness and consideration toward yourself? Many of us hold a deep-rooted belief that we don't deserve to be loved. *They* deserve friendship, but for some unfathomable reason *we* don't. This is a false belief. You *are* worthy of love. You *do* deserve your own support and friendship.

One reason we find it hard to befriend ourselves is that we can't forgive ourselves for what we see as our sins. When we evaluate our own performance in life, we immediately call forth memories of acts of kindness, courage, or thoughtfulness which we "should" have done, or of the "bad" things we did do.

Is that fair?

Forgiveness

The child in woman is her growing tip, alive throughout our life span. . . . One of the labors of adulthood is to befriend in ourselves those handicapped and underdeveloped parts of our nature which we have set aside.

—M.C. Richards

Of course, we *do* do things that require forgiveness. Doctor Elisabeth Kubler-Ross, a specialist in the field of death and dying, calls Earth "the hospital planet." We are all here to recover and heal. Each of us carries internal wounds. We all grope for what is right. Forgiveness creates an atmosphere in which we can heal.

Think frequently of your inner child. Treat her with gentleness, forgiveness, and tolerance. Whenever I fail, do something foolish, or feel a need to be forgiven, I very deliberately think of myself as "Susie." Reverting to my childhood name helps me to remember my inner little girl and to soften my attitude toward myself.

I once received a very helpful button from a minister. It said:

Which stands for *Please Be Patient With Me, God Isn't Finished With Me Yet!*

We are always talking to ourselves. In our minds, we create stories about ourselves based on our current experiences, as well as experiences from the past. Too often we cast ourselves in the role of bad girl—that schmucky little kid who never quite measured up; the one who needed to be perfect in order to deserve to live; the victim, the phony, the antagonist.

The people around us when we were young helped us create these stories. Many families have a "bad kid" and a "good kid," a "smart kid" and a "dumb kid," an "everybody's favorite" and a "black sheep," a "responsible kid" and a "baby."

We carry these labels into adulthood. But now we can re-choose and re-create our stories: we can begin to tell stories about ourselves that are positive, encouraging, tolerant, forgiving, gentle, hopeful, and loving.

COMPARE:

> Good grief, you forgot to mail that report (get a sitter, whatever)! Can't you remember anything! You're probably getting senile! You have been really stupid lately. You are either sick, or you're really losing it! You *should* be able to remember (_____)!

WITH:

> Susie, you are really forgetful lately.
> What's going on? Are you running on
> overload, feeling sick, or burning out?
> Maybe it's time to do something special
> for yourself.

The first story is very destructive. It lays the groundwork for fears of illness and failure and definitely isn't conducive to forgiveness. The second story is constructive and self-loving.

The subconscious is like wet clay: it retains the imprint of whatever we press into it, and it faithfully reproduces that imprint in our lives. If we tell ourselves stories that indicate that we don't deserve to be loved, to succeed, to lose weight, our subconscious will keep us unloved, failing, and chubby.

Tell yourself optimistic, realistic, and *friendly* stories. Avoid tragedies and grandiose fairy tales in which you play the goblin or the helpless victim. Sure, you may have warts (So do I! We all do!), but that makes you a candidate for healing, not a frog or a witch!

Support Systems: Everyone Needs Comfort

*Peace between countries must rest on the
solid foundation of love between individuals.*
—Gandhi

No one can heal your painful feelings but you, and it's almost impossible to heal them by yourself. We all need to be heard, to be valued, and to be guided. Often our noses are pressed so tightly against the map that we can't see the road to take. A good friend and confidant can be our best mirror—a clear and objective second pair of eyes in a muddled situation.

Isolation kills. We know from studies of orphaned children and animals that babies wither away if they aren't held and cuddled frequently. The clinical term for this wasting-away syndrome is "failure to thrive." Even as adults, without support systems we, too, fail to thrive.

Support is *not* one-sided. If we're to receive support, we must support others. Most of us, however, as women, wives, mothers, nurses, secretaries, and so on have been more supportive than supported.

A word of warning about supporting and being supported: a healthy source of support *cares* about your pain but does not *carry* it for you or try to *cure* it. Nor can you ever realistically expect to *carry* or *cure* another person's pain. It's easy to fall into the trap of passively expecting others to do all the healing work for us or to try to do all the work for someone else.

Watch for the signs of an unhealthy imbalance in your support relationships: fatigue and a feeling of being overloaded with other people's troubles or a tendency to avoid certain people and to feel impatient or angry with them. If you see these reactions in yourself, you may be carrying others' pain as if it were your own, perhaps even feeling total responsibility for saving them. What's happened is that you've neglected to honor your own limits and boundaries.

Conversely, if you feel abandoned, rejected, victimized, deserted, or angry at your support system (or part of it), ask yourself if you've been expecting those people to carry and cure your pain for you. Every person is responsible for his own pain. Feel *with* other people, not *for* them. Be a care-giver, not a cure-giver.

Expand your support systems. Treat yourself to several sources of comfort and guidance. Finding safe places and safe people takes time, but it's well worth the effort.

AWARE

> *To be contemplative is to be carefully and gently present to ourselves, not in unconscious self-absorption, but in quiet and loving observation.*
>
> —Marv Hiles

See yourself honestly and gently. You're not "finished" yet, and chances are you won't be finished within this one, short life span. Enjoy the *process* of re-creating and continually creating yourself.

ACKNOWLEDGE

With humor, tolerance, and forgiveness, allow yourself to be transparent to safe and accepting support systems that *care* for you and for which you care.

ACCEPT

Accept yourself and your becomingness with flexibility. The courage to be yourself is a quest, more easily accomplished in a climate of tolerance and acceptance.

Few of us live beyond
our three score and ten years,
and yet in that brief time
most of us create and live a unique biography
and weave ourselves into the fabric
of human history.

—ELISABETH KUBLER-ROSS

CHAPTER 16

Being Yourself: Honoring Your Past, Your Present, And Your Potential

NEITHER OUR PAST nor our present can describe our potential. Our potential is limitless: we use only a tiny fraction of our resources; the rest atrophies from fear, lack of self-acceptance, and the inability to dream.

To tap our vast potential for freedom and uniqueness, we must begin by honoring our past. Our past, whether it was securely nurturing or devastatingly destructive, gives us the *building blocks* with which we design our lives. If the building blocks were faulty, it is our job to transform them from *blocking* our way to *building* a free and satisfactory present.

The only moment of life we really "have" is the present—this minute, this hour, this day. All our opportunities beckon us from the center of *this moment*. *Today* we can improve on our choices. *Today* we can stand up for our rights. *Today* we can befriend ourselves.

As we work to become truly ourselves, each new day presents us with opportunities to unfold in the perfect right way.

The Past: Building blocks
The Present: Opportunities
The Future: Potential

A very wise woman once told me that the future depends on "a healed past and a well-lived present." Honor your present by living this day in a manner that will enable you to look back tomorrow with pride. Choose well today, and each day learn, from whatever sources inspire you, to love yourself just as you are—unfinished and still learning—and to live with your mate, family, co-workers and friends as a kind and considerate equal.

You have the right, the privilege, and the responsibility to be yourself *today*.

As you find the courage to be yourself and honor your integrity, your potential will be realized naturally. You'll develop an internal balance and harmony that will enable you to face any circumstance. You'll free yourself from limiting fears, and you'll be able to love and serve yourself and others from the overflow of your own abundance.

Be gentle with yourself. Becoming free is a lifelong process.

Our lives and feelings have a natural ebb and flow—a rhythm which we are often tempted to resist. You can no more successfully resist this rhythm than you could stop the ocean's ebb and flow. Far better to let the ocean ebb and, at low tide, take the opportunity to find wonders in the tide pools.

If you will allow *your* unique ebb and flow, your nights and days, the seasons of your soul, and find the courage to explore and heal your feelings at all levels of their tides, you will find treasures beyond belief: you will discover **The Courage To Be Yourself**.

> *Mother God, help me to be Loving*
> *Father God, help me to be Useful*
> *Mother/Father God, help me to be Me;*
> *a unique and valuable expression of You.*

Notes

Part I: The Courage To Be Yourself

page 3 Gloria Steinem, "Sisterhood" *The First Ms Reader* (1972)

Chapter 1: Courage: You Can Have It!

Page 6 Jane Fonda, "At Home With Tom and Jane" by Danae Brook, *LA Weekly* (1980)

Chapter 2: Getting There: A Road Map

page 12 Natasha Jasefowitz, *Is This Where I Was Going?* (New York: Warner Books, 1983) page 109

Part III: Unresolved Grief

Chapter 7: Debris

Chapter 8: The Leveled Life

Chapter 9: Natural Grief

Part IV: Limits And Boundaries

Chapter 10: Giving Ourselves Away

page 144   Virginia Woolf, *A Room of One's Own*, (New York: Harcourt, Brace & World, 1957)

page 149   Jordan and Margaret Paul, *Do I Have to Give Up Me to Be Loved by You?* (Minneapolis: CompCare Publications, 1983)

page 151   Charlotte Whitton, *Canada Month* (June 1963)

Chapter 11: Allowing Ourselves To Be Invaded

page 154   Colette Dowling, *The Cinderella Complex* (New York: Summit Books, 1981)

page 164   Gloria Steinem, *New Woman* (1987)

Chapter 12: Yes! We Do Have Rights!

page 168   Henrik Ibsen, "A Dolls House," *Four Great Plays* (New York: Bantam Books, 1959)

page 171   Erich Fromm

page 172   Agnes Repplier, *Books and Men* (1888)

page 175   Seneca Indian Saying

page 175   William Blake, *Collected Poems of William Blake* (1974)